Gary Skinner, Ken Crafer,
Melissa Turner and Ann Skinner

Cambridge IGCSE® and O Level

Environmental Management

Workbook

CAMBRIDGE
UNIVERSITY PRESS

CAMBRIDGE
UNIVERSITY PRESS

University Printing House, Cambridge CB2 8BS, United Kingdom

One Liberty Plaza, 20th Floor, New York, NY 10006, USA

477 Williamstown Road, Port Melbourne, VIC 3207, Australia

314–321, 3rd Floor, Plot 3, Splendor Forum, Jasola District Centre, New Delhi – 110025, India

103 Penang Road, #05-06/07, Visioncrest Commercial, Singapore 238467

Cambridge University Press is part of the University of Cambridge.

It furthers the University's mission by disseminating knowledge in the pursuit of education, learning and research at the highest international levels of excellence.

www.cambridge.org
Information on this title: www.cambridge.org/9781316634875

First published 2017

20 19 18 17 16 15 14 13 12 11 10

Printed in Great Britain by CPI Group (UK) Ltd, Croydon CR0 4YY

A catalogue record for this publication is available from the British Library

ISBN 978-1-316-63487-5 Paperback

All questions and sample answers have been written by the authors. Answers to the workbook exercises can be found on the Teacher's Resource CD-ROM.

Thanks to the following for permission to reproduce photographs:
Cover jose1983/Getty Images; page 16 Ken Crafer, page 49 KAMONRAT/Shutterstock; page 68 Gary Skinner/GJSSEC

....

Contents

Skills grid

This grid maps the workbook exercises to the Cambridge IGCSE® and O Level Environmental Management assessment objectives.

Assessment objectives	Key skills in Environmental Management	Workbook chapters								
		1	2	3	4	5	6	7	8	9
AO1 Knowledge with understanding										
1 Phenomena, facts, definitions, concepts and theories		1.1, 1.2, 1.5	2.1, 2.2, 2.3, 2.5	3.1, 3.2, 3.3, 3.4, 3.5, 3.6, 3.9, 3.10	4.2, 4.4, 4.5, 4.7, 4.8	5.1, 5.2, 5.3, 5.4	6.1, 6.3, 6.5	7.1, 7.2, 7.3, 7.4, 7.5	8.1, 8.2, 8.3, 8.4	9.1, 9.2, 9.3, 9.5, 9.6
2 Vocabulary, terminology and conventions		1.1, 1.5	2.1, 2.2	3.1, 3.2, 3.5, 3.9, 3.10	4.2, 4.4, 4.5, 4.7, 4.8	5.1, 5.2, 5.4	6.1, 6.3, 6.5	7.1, 7.2, 7.5	8.1, 8.3	9.1, 9.2, 9.5
3 Technological applications with their social, economic and environmental implications.		1.2, 1.3, 1.4	2.2, 2.4, 2.5, 2.6	3.7, 3.8	4.8		6.3	7.1, 7.3		9.6
AO2 Information handling and analysis										
1 Locate, select, organise and present information from a variety of sources	KS.4	1.4	2.2, 2.6	3.1, 3.6	4.8		6.2	7.2, 7.3, 7.4	8.1, 8.3	9.1, 9.3, 9.6
2 Translate information and evidence from one form to another	KS.3, KS.4	1.4	2.2, 2.3, 2.6	3.3, 3.4, 3.6, 3.7	4.3, 4.8	5.1, 5.2	6.2, 6.4	7.2	8.1	9.1, 9.3
3 Manipulate numerical data	KS.5	1.4	2.3, 2.4, 2.6	3.4, 3.6	4.1, 4.8	5.1, 5.3	6.2, 6.3, 6.4	7.2, 7.3, 7.4	8.1, 8.2, 8.3	9.1, 9.3, 9.4, 9.5, 9.6
4 Interpret and evaluate data, report trends and draw inferences.	KS.5		2.3, 2.4, 2.6	3.6, 3.9	4.8	5.2	6.2, 6.4	7.2, 7.4	8.1	9.1, 9.5

→

Assessment objectives	Key skills in Environmental Management	Workbook chapters								
		1	2	3	4	5	6	7	8	9
AO3 Investigation skills and making judgements										
1 Plan investigations	KS.1, KS.2	1.4	2.4	3.4	4.11	5.4	6.5	7.4		9.2
2 Identify limitations of methods and suggest possible improvements	KS.2, KS.6			3.4		5.4	6.5	7.4	8.1	
3 Present reasoned explanations for phenomena, patterns and relationships			2.1, 2.4	3.4, 3.9, 3.10	4.6, 4.7	5.3	6.2, 6.3, 6.4	7.2	8.1	9.1, 9.4, 9.6
4 Make reasoned judgements and reach conclusions based on qualitative and quantitative information.	KS.6	1.3, 1.4	2.4, 2.6	3.1, 3.4, 3.5, 3.9, 3.10	4.2, 4.3, 4.4, 4.6, 4.7, 4.8	5.1, 5.2, 5.4	6.2, 6.3, 6.4	7.2	8.1, 8.4	9.3, 9.4, 9.5, 9.6

v

Introduction

This book has been written to help you increase your understanding of the topics covered in your Cambridge IGCSE® or O Level Environmental Management course. The exercises in this workbook will give you opportunities to:

- develop your knowledge and understanding of different aspects of the course, including different phenomena, definitions and vocabulary

- practise handling information and solving problems

- develop your investigation and evaluation skills

- practise drawing and interpreting diagrams, including graphs.

Most of the exercises are somewhat different from examination questions. This is because they are designed to help you *develop* your knowledge, skills and understanding.

The Skills grid at the beginning of the book shows how each exercise maps to the course's assessment objectives. The first chapter focuses on developing your investigation and data handling skills. The rest of the chapters put more emphasis on your knowledge and understanding of the course content.

Each exercise starts with an introduction explaining the skills that it will help you to practise. Spaces have been left for you to write your answers. Some of the diagrams are incomplete, and your task will be to complete them.

Chapter 0:
Key skills in Environmental Management

In all IGCSE subjects, certain skills are examined in addition to the knowledge of the content of the syllabus. Science subjects, such as Environmental Management, involve a subset of skills which are dealt with in this chapter. These skills fall into two main categories:

- information handling and analysis
- investigation skills.

The following workbook questions focus on these two groups of skills. In addition, the coursebook questions will very often involve the use of these skills in the context of syllabus topics.

Exercise KS.1 Aims and hypotheses testing, experimental design

> The aim of the investigation identifies why it is being done. Once the aim has been decided, a hypothesis can be written. To test the hypothesis, scientists will most commonly design an experiment. An experiment is a situation in which one variable (x, the independent variable) is changed and its effect on another variable (y, the dependent variable) is measured. This exercise will help you to improve your understanding of experimental design. It will give you practice in formulating hypotheses.

1 a An investigation has the aim 'to investigate the effects of soil pH on the growth of plants near a mine waste tip'. Suggest a suitable null hypothesis for this investigation.

....

....

b Explain how you could collect data to decide whether the null hypothesis you have written can be accepted or rejected. That is, how would you test your hypothesis?

....

....

....

....

....

....

....

....

....

....

c An experiment was carried out and the following results were obtained.

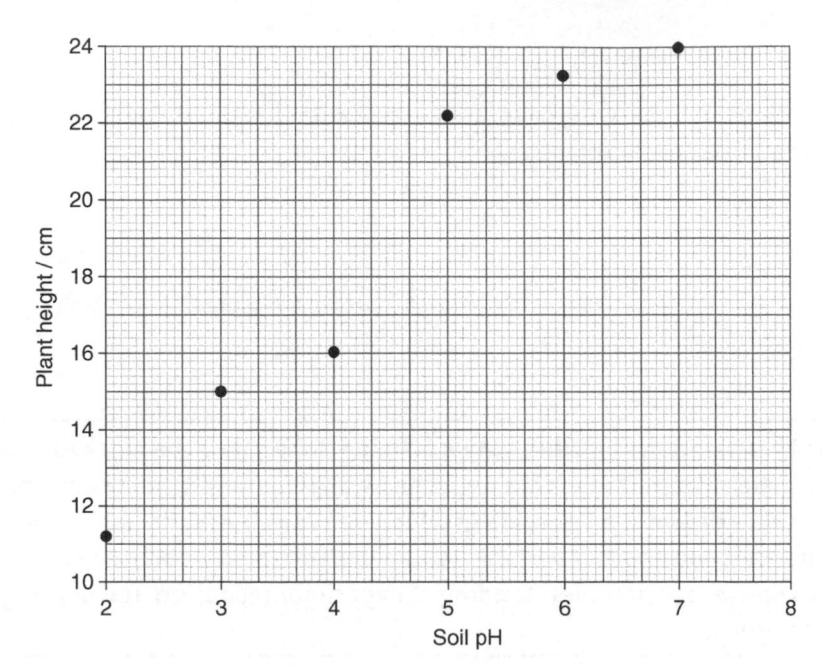

Describe the relationship between pH and plant height, and explain whether you think that the null hypothesis you have suggested in part a will be rejected or accepted in the light of these results.

....

....

....

....

....

2 An agricultural scientist was asked to find out if some heavy-metal pollution, which was getting into the irrigation water on some crop fields, was affecting crop growth. It was decided to do the experiment on plots outside rather than setting it up in pots in the laboratory.

A large field was chosen where no natural heavy-metal pollution was affecting the irrigation water. Four concentrations of the heavy metal were investigated. The field was divided into four plots. A maize crop was grown in each plot. Each plot was irrigated with pure water or water contaminated with the heavy metal. The total mass of maize cobs harvested was measured.

a Suggest an experimental hypothesis for this investigation.

....

....

....

b In this experiment, state the name of the independent variable and of the dependent variable.

independent variable ....

dependent variable ....

c Name **two** control variables in this experiment that are to do with the maize crop.

....

....

d Name **two** control variables in this experiment to do with the physical (abiotic) environment in which the maize is growing.

....

....

e Explain how the design of the experiment will ensure, as far as possible, that the variables you have named in part d will be the same in all four plots.

....

....

....

3

Exercise KS.2 Collecting data

> Data, in the context of a scientific experiment, will usually be numbers obtained from the experiment. It is important that you know what type of data have been obtained. There are two main types: quantitative and qualitative. Quantitative data can either be discrete or continuous and qualitative data is information that cannot be measured, like peoples' opinions. People's opinions can be expressed through some kind of interview, which can be structured in the form of a questionnaire. This exercise will help to improve your ability to select equipment for a stated purpose and design questionnaires. It will allow you to practise recognising different types of data.

1   The heavy-metal pollutant mentioned in Exercise KS. 1 question 2 (pages 2–3), was also found to be contaminating streams, rivers and lakes in the area. A zoologist was asked to look at the effect of this on fish growth and reproduction. The hypotheses which were tested were:

'the growth rate of fish will be lower in the presence of higher heavy-metal concentrations in the water'

and

'fish will produce fewer eggs in the presence of heavy metal in the water'.

a   Explain how you would make the measurements needed to test the first hypothesis.

....

....

....

....

....

....

....

b   The particular species of fish investigated produced very large numbers of quite small eggs. Counting all of the eggs produced by a single female fish would not be possible. Explain how you could get a good estimate of the total number of eggs being laid by female fish without having to count them all.

....

....

....

....

....

....

....

....

c i Circle the correct description of the data which will be obtained when testing the hypothesis about fish growth.

qualitative continuous quantitative continuous

qualitative discrete quantitative discrete

ii Circle the correct description of the data which will be obtained when testing the hypothesis about fish reproduction.

qualitative continuous quantitative continuous

qualitative discrete quantitative discrete

2 In a follow-up study, people in the area where heavy-metal pollution occurred were asked about their concerns using a questionnaire.

Here are some of the questions they were asked:

> **A** How concerned are you about the pollution of your water supply with heavy metals?
>
> **very concerned** **concerned** **don't know** **not concerned**
>
> **B** Please tell me about any incidents in which you think you were affected by using water polluted with heavy metal.
>
> **C** How much water do you drink in a day?
>
> **< 1 L** **about 1 L** **> 1 L**
>
> **D** Who do you blame for the heavy-metal pollution?

a There are two main types of questions in a questionnaire: closed questions and open questions. Which of questions A to D in the questionnaire do you think are open and which are closed?

open questions ....

closed questions ....

b   After the scientist wrote the questions shown, it was decided that the order in which they were asked could be improved. Suggest a better order for these questions and explain your answer.

....

....

c   Suggest **two** further questions that could be asked in this questionnaire. One of the questions should be closed and one should be open.

....

....

....

....

....

....

Exercise KS.3   Recording data

It is important to have a clear and sensible way of recording your data before starting an investigation. This exercise will give you some practice at deciding how to record results.

1   a   When counting the fish eggs in the investigation described in Exercise KS.2 question 1b (page 4), a tally chart was used. In one square 73 eggs were counted. Write down the tally chart record of this number of eggs.

b In the same investigation, seven concentrations of heavy metal, including zero, were used. The number of eggs laid by five females at each concentration was estimated. A mean number of eggs per female was then calculated. The heavy-metal concentrations were designated 0 to 6. Draw a table in which the results of this experiment could be recorded, together with the calculated mean.

Exercise KS.4 Presenting data

> There are many ways of presenting the data collected in an investigation. Ideally, it should be recorded in a table. Once the data is neatly presented in a table, it can be displayed. This will usually be in the form of a graph or chart. This exercise will help you to practise your graph plotting skills. It will also help you to choose which type of graph or chart to use for different kinds of data.

1 **a** In the investigation described to test the two hypotheses in Exercise KS.2 question 1 (pages 4–5), the data obtained were treated in two different ways. In one case the data were growth rates (expressed as gain in mass per day) and in the other the number of eggs. In both cases the scientist was looking at the effect of heavy-metal concentration on these variables.

There are generally five ways in which you might choose to present data. These are a line graph, a bar chart, a histogram, a pie chart and a scattergraph. State which of these you would use to present the data that were obtained to test the two hypotheses in Exercise KS.2 question 1 (pages 4–5). Explain why you have chosen this method.

....

....

....

....

....

....

....

....

....

....

b Another study was done which measured the percentage of various species of fish in which egg laying was reduced by the heavy-metal pollutants. The results are shown in the table.

Category of effect of heavy metal on fish egg laying	Percentage of fish species affected in this category
unaffected	7
slightly affected	23
significantly affected	52
very badly affected	18

State which of the data presentation techniques you would use to display these data. Explain your answer. Give an alternative method that would still be suitable.

....

....

....

....

....

c   The data on which this categorisation was based are shown below.

Number of eggs laid as a percentage of the number laid with no heavy-metal pollutant	Number of species laying this percentage of normal number of eggs
100–80	2
<80–60	15
<60–40	17
<40–20	29
<20–0	59

Calculate how many species of fish were investigated.

....

d   Explain which method of data presentation you would use with the data in part c. Explain your answer.

....

....

Exercise KS.5 Analysing data

When analysing the data you have collected and presented, you should be doing one or more of a number of possible things:

- looking for trends

- looking for patterns

- looking for associations

- calculating means, modes and/or medians

- working out the range.

This exercise will help you to practise these skills.

1 a Look at the diagram below and describe

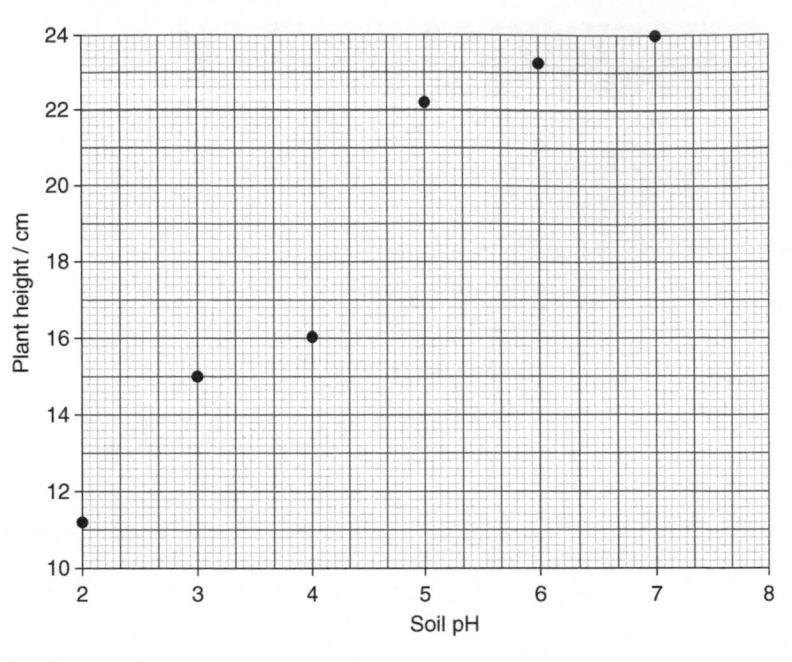

i the trend shown

....

....

....

ii the patterns shown.

....

....

....

b In the study in which five females were investigated at each of seven heavy-metal concentrations (see Exercise KS.3, pages 6–7) the following results were found at a heavy-metal concentration of 2.

Female 1: 79 eggs, Female 2: 98 eggs, Female 3: 64 eggs, Female 4: 90 eggs, Female 5: 79 eggs.

Calculate the mean, the median, the mode and the range of these data.

mean ....

median ....

mode ....

range ....

Exercise KS.6 Drawing conclusions and evaluating

In an experimental investigation, the conclusion usually involves deciding whether the null hypothesis can be rejected or accepted. You should be able to give reasons for the decision you make.

The evaluation involves looking for any problems with the investigation and, most importantly, suggesting how they might be solved. This exercise will give you a chance to practise drawing conclusions and evaluating.

1 **a** Looking back through all the data in this workbook chapter, explain whether you think it is justifiable to state that the heavy-metal pollution causes a reduction in both the growth rate and reproductive capacity of fish. Give reasons for your decision.

....

....

....

....

....

....

b Suggest how the experiment which looks at the effect of pH on plant growth (Exercise KS.1, pages 1–3) could be improved and extended.

....

....

....

....

....

Chapter 1:
Rocks and minerals and their exploitation

This chapter covers the following topics:

- how different rock types are formed – the rock cycle
- methods of extracting rocks and minerals
- the impacts of rock and mineral extraction
- managing the impact of rock and mineral extraction
- sustainable use of rocks and minerals.

Exercise 1.1 The rock cycle

> This exercise will help you to understand the basics of the rock cycle, including important terms.

1 Insert these words into the correct spaces on the diagram.

igneous rocks   sedimentary rocks   weathering

metamorphic rocks   transportation   magma

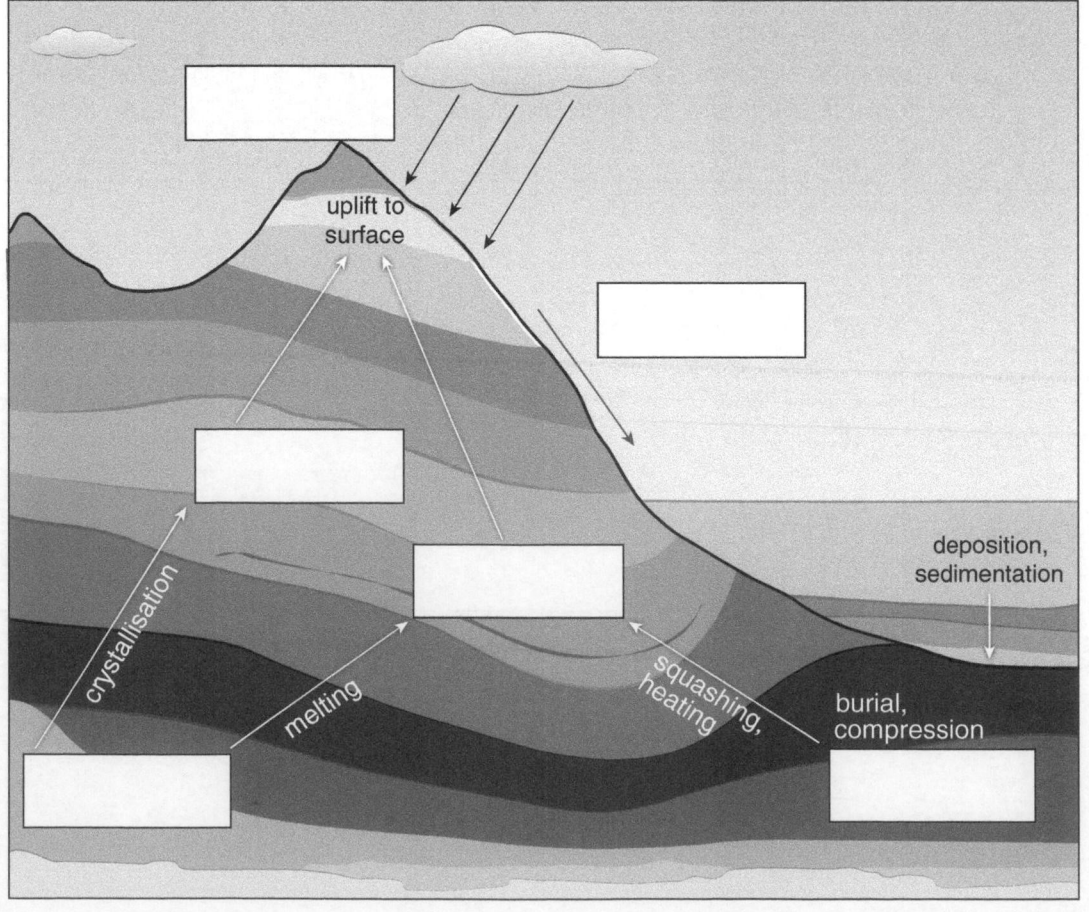

2 Complete this 'Yes/No' decision chart (also known as a key) to allow a young student to be able to find out what rock they are looking at from the list below.

Decision chart

1 Does the rock have lines or strata?   If YES go to 2. If NO go to 3

2 Does the rock have extremely small or invisible grains?   If YES go to 4. If NO go to 5

3 Does the rock contain crystals?   If YES go to 6. If NO go to 7

4

5

6

7

8

9

10

Rock types

basalt   limestone   sandstone

marble   slate   granite   shale

3 Draw lines to link the following 'M' words with their correct definitions.

magma	Naturally occurring inorganic substances with a specific chemical composition
mineral	Molten rock below the surface of the Earth
metamorphic	An example of a metamorphic rock
marble	Rocks formed from existing rocks by a combination of heat and pressure

4 Describe how a sedimentary rock forms.

....

....

....

....

....

Exercise 1.2 Extracting rocks and minerals

Rocks and minerals are valuable resources: their discovery in the ground and their location will affect the way they are extracted. This exercise will help you to understand these processes.

1   Describe **three** methods used to search for deposits of minerals that may be found in the Earth.

....

....

....

....

....

....

2   A new source of minerals has been found. It is decided that the minerals should be extracted from this new source. Explain how the following three factors might affect the way the minerals might be extracted.

Geology

....

....

....

....

Environmental impact

....

....

....

....

Market price for the minerals

....

....

....

3 Complete the table to identify the advantages and disadvantages of these different types of mining.

Mine type	Advantages	Disadvantages
Open pit mining		
Strip mining		
Drift mining		
Shaft mining		

Exercise 1.3 The impacts of rock and mineral extraction

This exercise will help you to understand the impacts of rock and mineral extraction on local communities and ecosystems.

The photo shows part of a stone quarry. The quarry produces large blocks of stone that will be carved for important buildings.

1   How might the extraction of this stone be of benefit to the local people?

   ....

   ....

   ....

   ....

   ....

   ....

2   Describe **three** negative impacts the development of this quarry could have on the local community.

....

....

....

....

....

....

3   Suggest **three** ways in which the local ecosystem might be affected by the development of the quarry.

....

....

....

....

....

....

4   The removal of topsoil has resulted in the local extinction of a small flowering plant. Suggest why this loss may be important.

....

....

....

....

5   Which of the **four** extraction methods listed in Exercise 1.2 question 3 (page 15), is likely to have the least impact on a rare plant? Give a reason for your answer.

....

....

....

....

Exercise 1.4 Managing the impact of rock and mineral extraction

Minerals are a finite resource. Global demand for minerals is increasing, putting additional pressures on habitats and local areas. This exercise will help you to evaluate different ways in which this impact can be managed and will help you to apply these principles to new or unfamiliar scenarios.

1   A mining company has the responsibility to ensure that a mining site is left in good condition once excavation has been completed. This is often planned before a licence will be granted to allow extraction from a site.

Give an evaluation of the suitability of the following proposals for an old site with a large bowl-like crater. Make sure that you include the strengths and weakness of each proposal.

The diagram shows an old mining site which now needs to have another purpose.

Potential use	Evaluation
Waste disposal site for household waste	
Naturalising the area by planting trees and sowing wild flower seeds	
Conversion of the crater into a race track	
Flood the crater for use as a fish farm	
Develop a shopping centre in the crater	

2   Describe a way the waste from mining activities could be disposed of safely. Describe the checks the mining company should do to ensure that the waste materials are not causing damage to the local environment.

....

....

....

....

....

....

3   Mining companies will often include tree planting in their plans for the restoration of a site. It is often observed that the growth of these trees is very slow compared to trees planted at other sites.

Suggest reasons why this might be the case.

....

....

....

....

....

....

4 Tree planting can be labour intensive. In Canada, a company pays $0.11 for each young tree planted as part of its reforestation programme.

How much would a worker earn if they planted 1600 trees per day?

....

5 It is estimated that only about 40% of the young trees in question 4 survive for more than 5 years. How many trees will survive for more than 5 years from one worker's day of planting?

....

6 A manager plans to look at the survival rate of trees to see whether the percentage could be increased. Outline an investigation that could be done to evaluate whether additional training given to tree planters would have an effect.

....

....

....

....

....

....

....

....

Exercise 1.5 The sustainable use of rocks and minerals

The price of most rocks and minerals is increasing as the supply is limited and demand is increasing. This exercise will help you to understand many of the key terms and definitions used when describing sustainable use and extraction.

1   Fill in the words in this puzzle to reveal a method that organisations can use to help ensure mineral resources are used appropriately. (Some of the letters in each word have been put in to help you.)

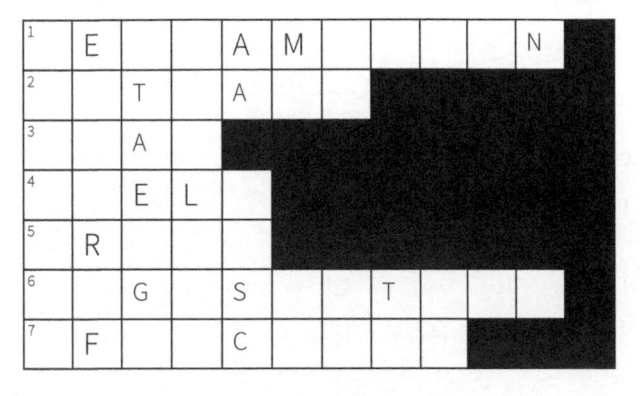

1   The method of collecting, extracting and re-using scrap metal. (11)

2   Removing the useful metal from ore. (7)

3   A widely mined fossil fuel. (4)

4   The percentage of a mineral obtained from the rock. (5)

5   The method of breaking down large rocks into smaller pieces to obtain the minerals. (5)

6   A way that a government can control the use and extraction of minerals. (11)

7   The effective use of extracted minerals. (9)

2   Suggest **four** reasons why the amount of recycled metals used in industry may be less than the amount potentially available.

....

....

....

....

....

....

....

3 Give **three** ways a government might ensure that a higher proportion of metals in the home are recycled.

....

....

....

....

....

....

4 Give **two** reasons why people in certain neighbourhoods might consider an increase in the recycling of metals to be a poor idea.

....

....

....

....

Energy and the environment

This chapter covers the following topics:

- fossil fuels
- energy resources
- the demand for energy
- conservation and management of energy resources
- impact of oil pollution
- management of oil pollution.

Exercise 2.1 Fossil fuels

> Understanding the processes that allow fossil fuels to form is fundamental knowledge. This exercise will help to embed the basic concepts in your mind.

1   Use words from this list to complete the passage about fossil fuels and their formation.

organic	plants	pressure
sediment	ground	coal

Fossil fuels are not actually made from fossils, but it is a useful term to describe the amount of

time it takes to produce them. Fossils fuels are produced from the decay of ....

and animals. These remains formed .... matter that became covered

in layers of ....

Over millions of years, and buried deep in the .... by the addition of further

layers of sediment, the organic material is subjected to high .... and heat.

The precise conditions, and the type of animal and plant material available, will determine whether

...., oil or natural gas is produced.

2 Explain why it is not possible to produce more coal or oil simply by collecting and composting organic waste matter, which is easily available.

....

....

....

....

3 Why are fossil fuels normally found buried under deep layers of rock?

....

....

Exercise 2.2 Energy resources

This exercise will help to develop your skills in identifying the type of energy source that is being used. It is important to be able to classify renewable and non-renewable sources correctly.

1 Organise the following energy sources into the columns of the table.

oil   geothermal   hydroelectric   wave

coal   nuclear   tidal   natural gas

wind   solar   biofuels

Non-renewable energy sources	Renewable energy sources

2   Describe how a wind turbine may be used to produce electricity.

....

....

....

....

3   Solar power is often used as an energy generation source. It is also used in the home to provide light. How else might solar energy be used in the home?

....

....

4   Renewable energy schemes are not always popular. Complete the table by giving a reason; economic, social or environmental, why people might not be in favour of a new renewable energy scheme in their area.

Issue	Reason given
Economic	
Social	
Environmental	

Exercise 2.3 The demand for energy

This exercise will help you to explore the factors affecting the demand for energy and how factors such as the world economy have an impact on overall demand. These are complex subjects and will need some careful thought.

1 How will the following changes affect the demand for energy? Tick the correct box for each.

	Increase	Remain the same	Decrease
A change in employment types in a country from farming to industrial			
A downturn in the world economy			
Increased average household wages			
A warmer than expected winter temperature in a temperate country			
The building of a more affordable car in an LEDC			
A law meaning power companies must use more renewable sources of energy			
An increase in population			

2 The table below shows an estimate of the annual amount of power used by twelve countries. To make a fair comparison, the total power used in a country has been divided by the population size. This gives the average power consumption for a citizen of that country. The highest usage would be ranked 1 and the lowest ranked 12.

Country	Power use (average per person)/GJ
Afghanistan	3.78
Angola	30.09
Australia	234.92
Bangladesh	8.77
Belgium	234.59
Cambodia	14.93
India	23.76
Japan	163.73
Qatar	537.58
United Arab Emirates	347.40
United States of America	300.91
Zambia	26.37

a Complete the two tables.

Greatest users of power (per head of population)

Rank	Country
1	
2	
3	

Smallest users of power (per head of population)

Rank	Country
10	
11	
12	

b Describe the similarity between the countries using the least amount of power per person.

....

....

....

....

c Suggest reasons why the countries at the top of the ranking use so much energy per person.

....

....

....

....

d Using this data, calculate how many people from Afghanistan could be supplied with the power consumed by one person in Australia.

....

Exercise 2.4   Conservation and management of energy resources

As global energy demand increases, methods to use it more efficiently and reduce the level of waste become more important. The skills you will learn in this exercise can be applied to a lot of different situations.

1   The global demand for energy is increasing and many potential sources are limited in their supply. A household could become more energy efficient by reducing consumption and reducing energy waste. Give **two** examples of how energy consumption can be reduced, **two** examples of how energy waste can be reduced, and **two** examples of how energy can be re-used.

Reduce energy consumption

....

....

Reduce energy waste

....

....

Re-use energy

....

....

2 An analysis of the use of energy in a public building is shown in the diagram.

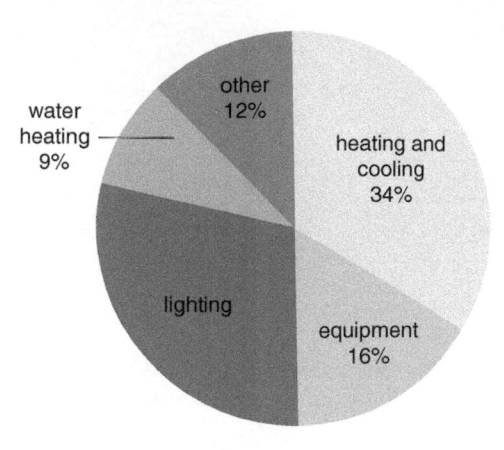

a Calculate the percentage of the energy which is used in lighting the building.

....

b The building uses $120 000 of energy per year. What is the cost of the energy used to power the equipment?

....

c It has been calculated that the offices in the building are wasting 9% of the energy supplied to equipment because it is left in 'standby' mode when not in use.

How much money would be saved if staff were made to switch items off?

....

d Suggest **two** ways in which the building could be modified in order to reduce the amount of energy used on heating and cooling.

....

....

....

....

3 Energy companies are being encouraged to generate an increasing proportion of their electricity from renewable sources. Why might the use of non-renewable resources still have a significant part to play for many years to come?

....

....

....

....

4 A plan has been submitted to allow the extraction of oil by fracking (hydraulic fracturing). The local community group is against the plan.

Produce an explanation of the benefits of fracking that could be used to highlight the benefits of this plan.

....

....

....

....

....

....

5 A student plans to investigate the energy use of three different types of light bulb that are commonly used in buildings.

a Outline the equipment and method they will need to use to complete this investigation.

....

....

....

....

....

....

....

....

b The information from this investigation can be used to calculate the cost of energy used by each type of light bulb.

Explain which other factors need to be included in this calculation to be able to evaluate the true costs of each type of light bulb.

....

....

....

....

....

....

Exercise 2.5 Impact of oil pollution

This exercise will help you to develop the appropriate vocabulary relating to the subject of oil pollution.

1 Answer the clues to complete the puzzle. Each question relates to an aspect of oil pollution.

When complete, the name of a famous oil spill accident will appear.

1 An unintended or unexpected incident. (8)

2 The sea environment. (6)

3 Location of many oil rigs. (8)

4 Name to describe unrefined oil. (5)

5 Liquid fossil fuel. (3)

6 The reason for many oil tanker spills. (9)

7 Excluded from the sea when the sea is covered in oil. (3)

8 The impact of an oil spill on many organisms. (5)

9 An oil spill will severely effect a local tourism .... (8)

10 The ideal number of oil spills. (4)

Name of oil spill accident ....

2 Explain why onshore oil spills have a far smaller impact when compared to those that occur in the sea.

....

....

....

....

Exercise 2.6 Management of oil pollution

> The world is very reliant on oil. There are huge challenges in transporting it from the areas where it is located to other countries that use large amounts. This exercise will help explore these issues.

The graph below shows the number of oil transport movements between 1970 and 2014, and the number of major oil spills during the same period.

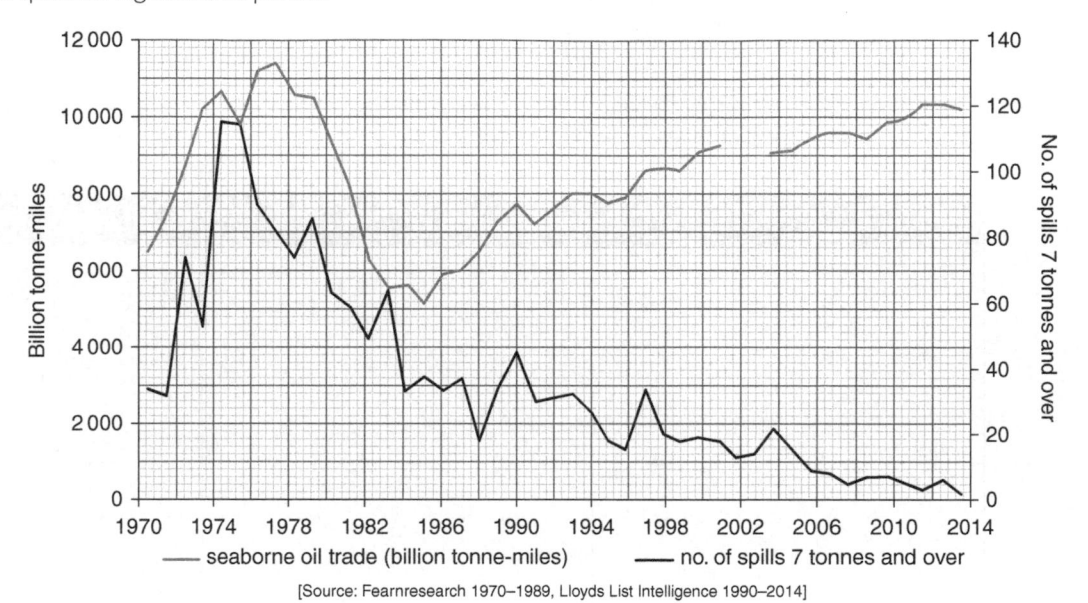

—— seaborne oil trade (billion tonne-miles)　　—— no. of spills 7 tonnes and over

[Source: Fearnresearch 1970–1989, Lloyds List Intelligence 1990–2014]

1　Complete the graph by plotting the data for the seaborne oil trade for 2003 : 7800 billion tonne-miles.

2　In what year was there the greatest number of major oil spills?

....

....

3　Describe the trends in the amount of oil transport movement taking place.

....

....

....

....

4　What changes to tanker design might be responsible for the trend in major oil spills?

....

....

5 In 1983, the MARPOL treaty was introduced. This has helped in reducing the number of major oil spills. Why was the drop in incidents gradual and not immediate?

....

....

....

....

6 Accidents will still mean that spillages occur. Give **three** ways in which a spill may be cleared up, and give the advantages and disadvantages for each method.

Method	Advantage	Disadvantage

Chapter 3:
Agriculture and the environment

This chapter covers the following topics:

- the composition of soil
- the components needed in soil for plant growth
- understanding the availability and effect of soil nutrients
- comparing the use and properties of clay and sandy soils
- classifying types of agriculture
- improving agricultural yield
- controlling the growing environment
- impacts on the environment
- managing soil erosion
- sustainable farming.

Exercise 3.1 The composition of soil

> Knowledge of the composition of the soil is a fundamental building block in successfully understanding the topic. Understanding key terms is an important skill in helping to develop an appropriate vocabulary. This exercise will give you practice in both these areas.

1 Use words from this list to complete the information about soil composition.

mineral	organic	increase	weathering
habitat	four	decrease	pores

Soil is a .... for plants and other organisms. The ....

main components of soil are: .... particles, the ....

content, air and water. The proportion of air in the soil will depend on the size of the ....

in the soil and the amount of water in the soil at any particular time. In drought conditions, the amount of air

will .... and water content ....

The mineral particles occupy the largest volume of the soil and are formed from the parent rocks by

.... and erosion.

2   Sort the following particles and their characteristics into the table below. Start with the **largest** particles.

Silt   <0.002mm   silky

Sand   2.0–0.02mm   sticky

Clay   0.02–0.002mm   gritty

Particle	Size of particle (mm)	Texture (when moist)

3   A student has decided to investigate the components of a soil by adding a sample to a jar, adding water, shaking it well and allowing it to settle. Explain what they are likely to see after 15 minutes.

....

....

....

....

Exercise 3.2 Components needed in soil for plant growth

The mineral fraction is only one component that makes up a fertile soil. There are many others. This exercise will help you to explore these different items.

1   Fill in the across clues in this puzzle to reveal the name of one of the three major nutrients needed by plants for successful growth.

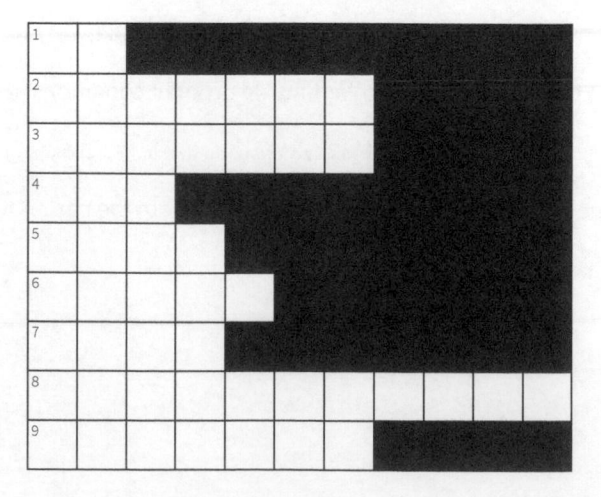

1 Scale on which the acidity of the soil is measured. (2)

2 Description of the part of the soil that is composed of living organisms and their remains. (7)

3 Word to describe the feel of a soil. (7)

4 A variable component of the soil, the amount of this in the soil is affected by the water content. (3)

5 The largest of the three mineral soil particle types. (4)

6 A word to describe the feel of silt particles when rubbed between your fingers. (5)

7 Minor plant nutrient which causes a yellowing of the leaves between the veins if there is a shortage of this nutrient in the plant. (4)

8 What certain plant nutrients may become in the soil at the incorrect acidity levels. (11)

9 The component of the soil which is a combination of rock fragments and other non-living items. (7)

Plant nutrient: ………………………………

Exercise 3.3 Understanding the availability and effect of soil nutrients

> **Plants need a range of nutrients (mineral ions) to enable them to grow healthily. A shortage of any of these will reduce the growth and ultimate yield of the plant. In some cases, too much of a nutrient may also be damaging the plant; possibly causing too much (weak) growth or even being toxic to the plant.**
>
> **Describing plant nutrient deficiencies is a hard task to master. It will take a lot of practice as many symptoms are very similar. This exercise will help you.**

The availability of nutrients is affected by the pH (acidity or alkalinity) of the soil. The pH affects the roots' ability to take up these key nutrients. The diagram shows these relationships.

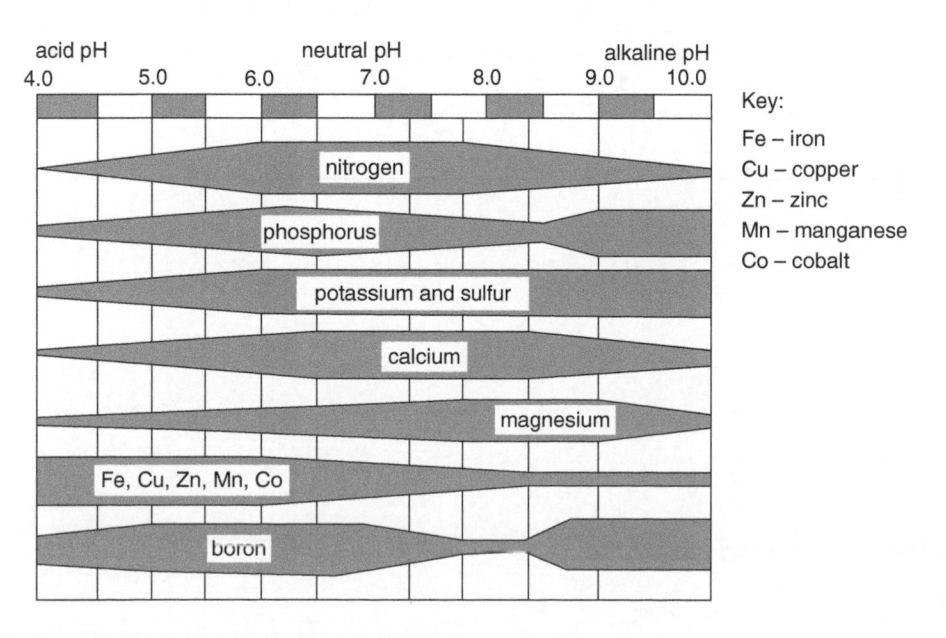

1   Which nutrients (mineral ions) are likely to be in short supply in a soil of pH 6.0?

....

....

....

....

2   What soil pH is likely to mean that the majority of minerals are available to the plant?

....

....

3   Complete the table, putting the plant nutrient next to its deficiency symptoms. Some have been done for you.

Calcium (Ca)   Copper (Cu)   Iron (Fe)   Potassium (K)   Zinc (Zn)

Plant nutrient	Symptoms of deficiency include
Nitrogen (N)	Slow growth, yellowing leaves (oldest first).
Phosphorus (P)	Leaves dull with blue-green colour. Leaves fall early.
	Poor-quality fruits and seeds, leaves with brown edges.
Sulfur (S)	Yellowing of leaves (youngest first).
	Death of plant tissues. Poor fruit storage.
Magnesium (Mg)	Yellowing of leaves between the leaf veins. Early leaf fall.
	Yellowing of leaves between the veins (youngest leaves first). Failure to flower.
	Dark green leaves become twisted and withered (young leaves first).
	Leaves show poor development, might only grow to a very small size.
Boron (B)	Leaves misshapen and malformed. Hard 'woody' areas in fruits and other storage organs.

Exercise 3.4 Comparing the use and properties of clay and sandy soils

Different crops need different growing conditions and therefore it is important for the farmer to use the properties of their soil to meet the needs of particular crops. This exercise compares the use and properties of clay and sandy soils.

1   Here are some soil properties. Add the letters for the properties in the correct boxes in the table below.

a   Excess water drains easily.

b   Nutrients leach through the soil more easily.

c   Risk of getting waterlogged.

d   Soil goes very hard when dry.

e   Soil is easier to cultivate.

f   Larger water holding capacity.

g   Soil warms up quicker (as holds less water).

	Advantages	Disadvantages
Clay soil		
Sandy soil		

2   A grower in a temperate climate wants to produce a crop as quickly as possible in the spring. Explain, with reasons, which soil type from the table above would be the better choice.

....

....

3   Another farmer is planning to grow a heavy-yielding crop that will require a lot of water and fertilisers. Which of the two soil types above should they choose? Justify your answer.

....

....

....

4   A soil has been analysed and found to contain 10% clay and 15% silt. What amount of sand is present in this soil, and what properties would it be expected to have?

....

....

....

5   Students are investigating the impact that soil type has on the root growth of a type of soybean.

They have been given:

- three soil types: a very sandy type, a soil with a high clay content and a loam soil

- three soy beans

- three identical glass jars.

a   Design an investigation using this equipment to investigate root growth of soybeans in different soil types.

....

....

....

....

....

....

....

b Suggest **three** improvements that could be made to make the results more reliable.

....

....

....

....

....

....

Exercise 3.5 Classifying types of agriculture

There are a number of ways of describing methods of farming. It is possible to see many types in a range of locations across the world. This exercise will help you to classify types of agriculture.

1 Match the correct term to its description.

extensive production	A farming system which both rears livestock and grows crops.
intensive production	A farming system that produces a relatively small amount from a large area of land.
arable farming	A farming system that focuses on breeding and rearing livestock.
pastoral farming	A farming system that produces large amounts from small areas of land.
mixed farming	A farming system that supplies food for the farmers and their families.
commercial farming	A farming system that focuses on the production of crops.
subsistence farming	A farming system where the majority of the food is sold to others.

2 The trend in much of the Western world is for agriculture to become more specialist whereas traditional agricultural systems produce a far wider range of crops. Suggest why these changes have occurred.

....

....

....

....

....

....

Exercise 3.6 Improving agricultural yield

Using the understanding of soils and production types, it is possible to investigate techniques to improve overall yield and efficiency from the land. You should be able to apply this knowledge to different situations. Even if a particular crop or animal species is unfamiliar, the same general principles will apply. This exercise will help you to develop your knowledge and skill in this area.

1 Give **three** reasons why farmers are being encouraged to increase the yield (amount of food) they are obtaining from their farms.

....

....

....

....

....

....

2 The table below shows an estimate of the amount of rice produced in China between 1950 and 2010. Plot the results as a graph.

Year	Yield of rice (million tonnes)
1950	55
1960	60
1970	110
1980	140
1990	189
2000	188
2010	195

3 Describe the trends in the graph.

....

....

....

....

....

....

4 Suggest **two** reasons for the result recorded in 2000.

....

....

....

....

5 Calculate the percentage change in yield between 1950 and 2010. Show your working.

....

6 Explain how the following techniques might be useful in increasing yield.

    a crop rotation

    ....

    ....

    ....

    ....

    b irrigation

    ....

    ....

    ....

    ....

    c plant breeding

    ....

    ....

    ....

    ....

    d pesticides

    ....

    ....

    ....

    ....

e herbicides (weed killers)

....

....

....

....

f mechanisation

....

....

....

....

g genetic modification

....

....

Exercise 3.7 Controlling the growing environment

Investment in technology is one way of helping to maximise yield. This exercise will help you to explore the ways in which the environment may be controlled.

Protected structures such as greenhouses are expensive to build but allow the grower to control all the growing conditions needed by the plant.

1   The diagram below shows a greenhouse structure with the conditions that can be controlled. For each of these conditions, complete the boxes with **two** different ways in which each factor could be managed by the grower.

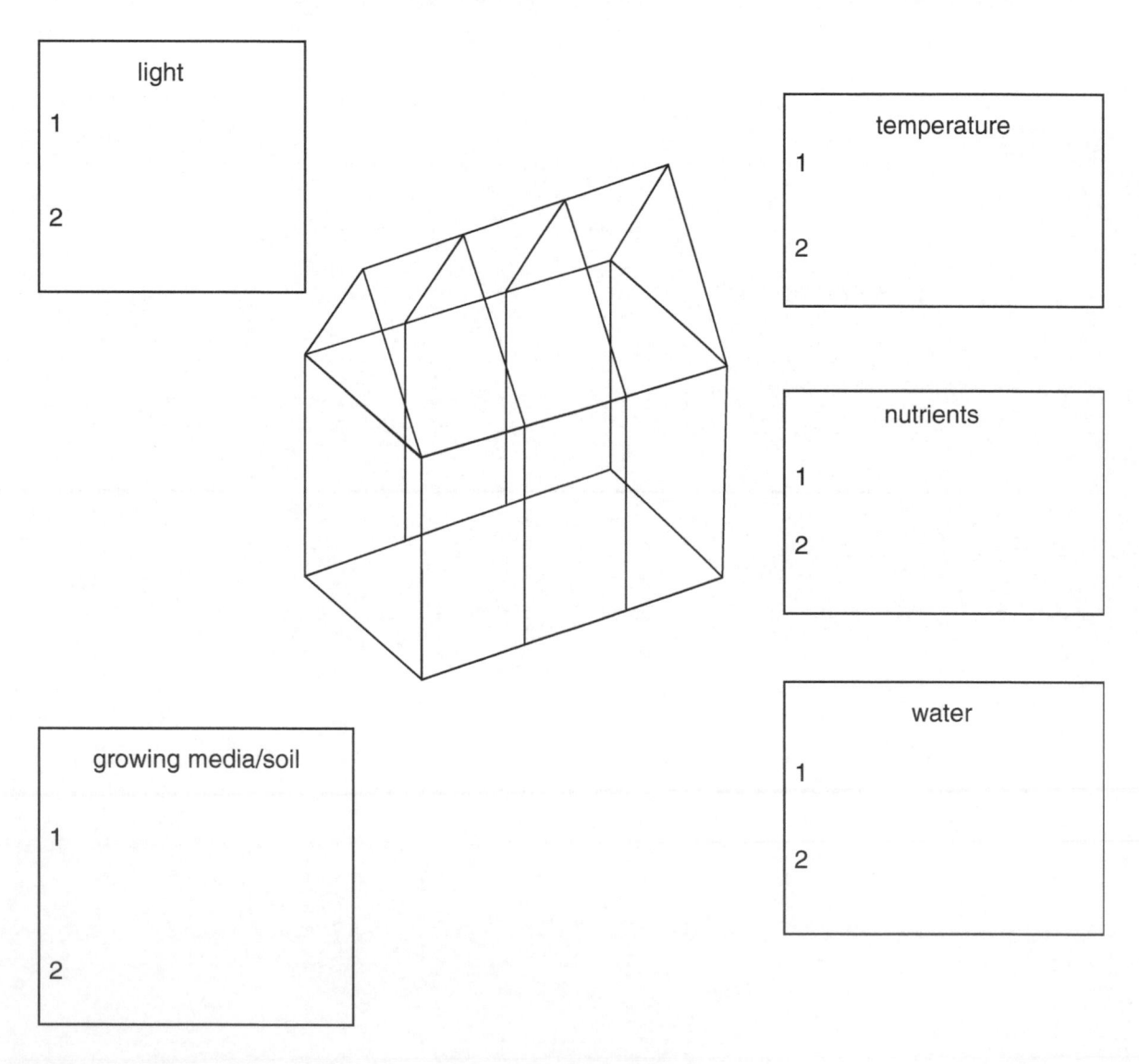

light

1

2

temperature

1

2

nutrients

1

2

growing media/soil

1

2

water

1

2

Exercise 3.8 Impacts on the environment

Managing the soil to increase yields uses a lot of resources (inputs) as part of the production system. Too much of any input risks damage to the environment. This is of great importance and therefore are key principles to be able to understand and apply. This exercise will help you to understand and apply these key principles.

1   Complete the table, which summarises some of the problems that may be caused by different inputs. (Some inputs may cause more than one problem.)

Production input	Name of potential problem	Definition of the problem
fertilisers	eutrophication	
irrigation		The increase in salt levels in the soil. This prevents plants from absorbing water efficiently through their roots.
	resistance	The lack of effectiveness of chemicals to kill plant pests due to over-use and mutation of the pests.
mechanisation	soil compaction	
irrigation	soil capping	
keeping grazing animals at high density		Reduction in amount of vegetation, loss of plant species, lack of plant roots causes erosion.
mechanisation	deforestation	

Exercise 3.9 Managing soil erosion

Loss of fertility is caused by a number of poor management techniques; the management of topsoil is key to helping maintain an appropriate farming environment. Failure to do so has multiple environmental consequences. This exercise will help you to understand how soil erosion can be managed.

Scientists are concerned about the rate of soil erosion occurring worldwide. Research shows that it takes many years for soils to be re-formed within an area once it has been lost.

1   Using the map, describe the degradation of soil across the world.

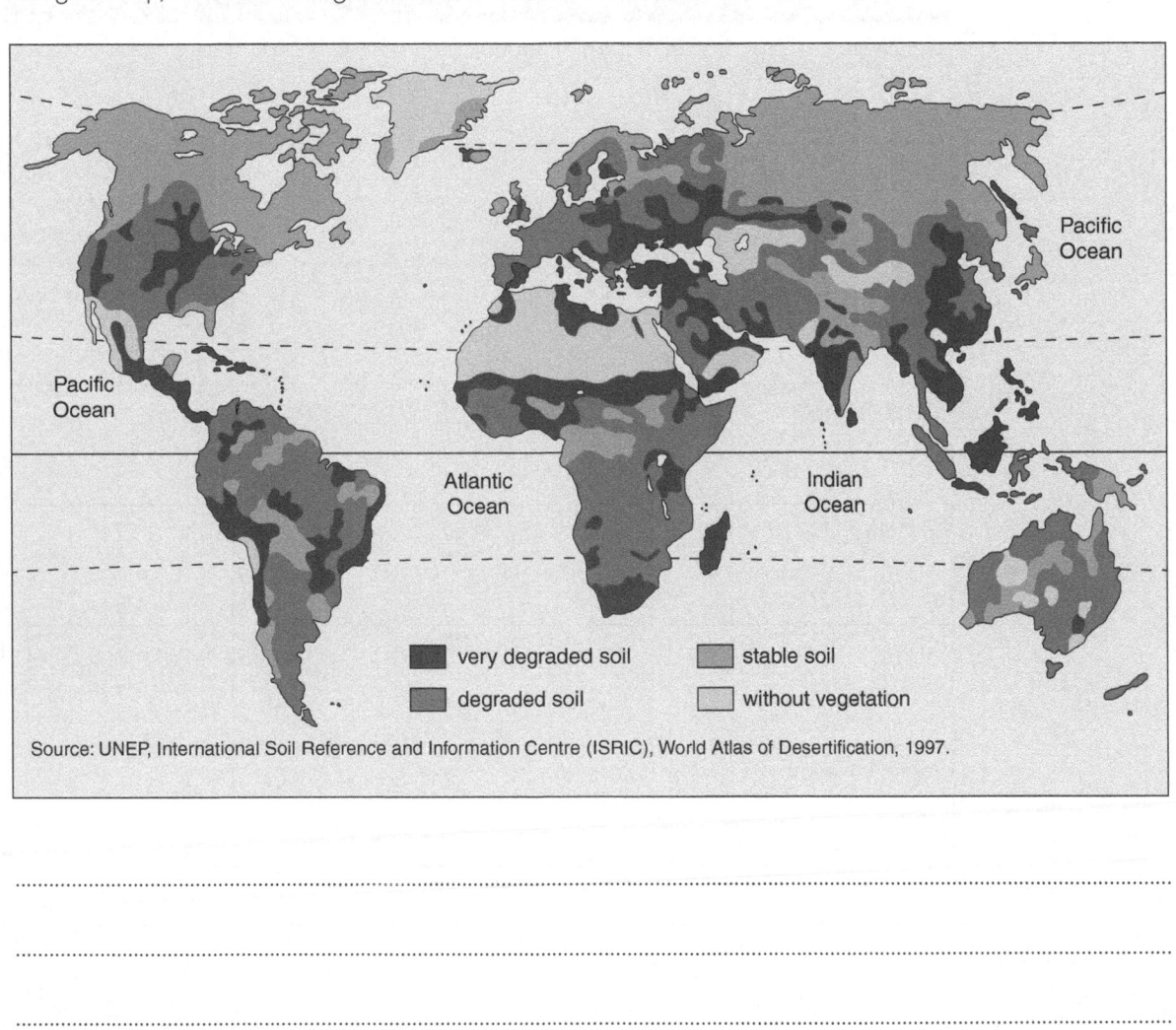

Source: UNEP, International Soil Reference and Information Centre (ISRIC), World Atlas of Desertification, 1997.

....

....

....

....

....

2 Suggest reasons for the location of the main areas which are marked as having 'stable soil'

....

....

....

....

3 The photograph shows the impact of erosion to a field caused by excessive water flow.

What impacts could this erosion have, both in the field and further downstream?

Impacts in the field	
Impacts downstream	

4 Excessive water is only one cause of soil erosion. Complete the boxes of the spider diagram with other reasons for erosion.

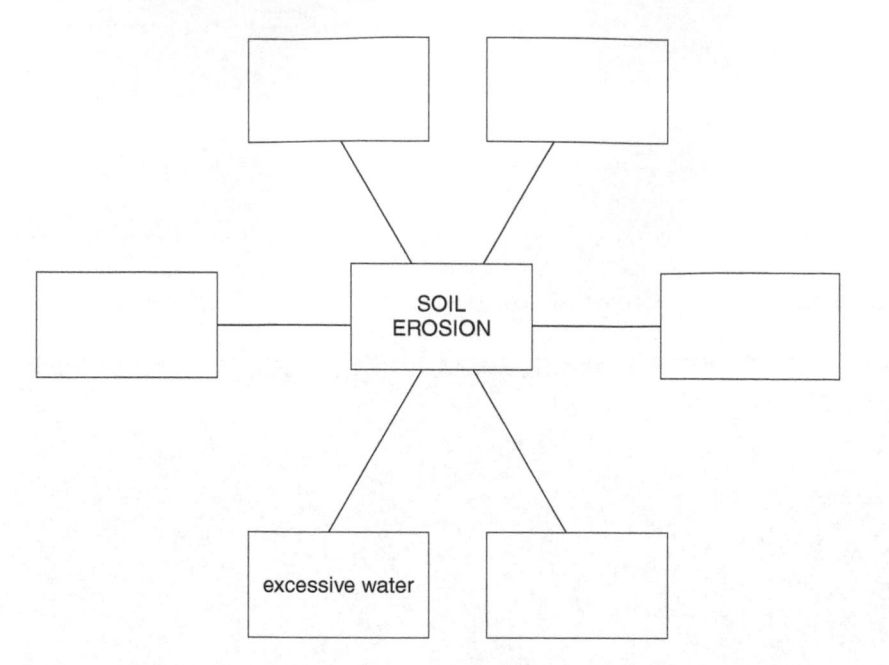

5 There are a number of ways of helping to reduce the risk of soil erosion. Complete the paragraphs below, using the correct words from the list.

terracing   infiltrate   topsoil   contours

bunds   roots   famine   permeable

Farmers need to cultivate land efficiently if they are to maximise its yield. If the techniques used result in

the loss of the ...., fertility is lost. One way in which the impact of erosion

on a steep slope may be reduced is by .... This reduces the speed of the

water and allows it to .... into the soil. Contour ploughing works on a similar

principle, the ridges and troughs following the .... of the land. The use of

....; artificial banks at the edges of growing spaces will also help hold

back water.

Wind erosion may also be reduced by planting natural vegetation at the edges of fields to act as wind breaks.

These act as .... barriers which reduce the speed of the wind. There are

numerous other ways of helping to reduce erosion. Leaving soil covered with the vegetation from a crop, for

example, will mean that soil is retained by the .... of the plants. Bare soil

increases the risk of erosion. Lack of topsoil may increase the risk of desertification in an area, increasing

.... and malnutrition to the local population.

6   Another method of helping reduce the risk of soil erosion is to increase the amount of organic matter. This helps improve the health and quality of the soil by the addition of humus, which helps stabilise smaller soil particles and acts like a sponge to hold additional water.

Here are some possible additions to the soil. Circle those that will add organic matter.

animal manure	clay	composted plant material	food waste
dead leaves	recycled paper	sand	chalk

Exercise 3.10 Sustainable farming

> **Scientists realise that, while there is a need to increase food production, this has to be achieved in a responsible manner. These questions will help develop your skills in being able to apply these key principles.**

1   Which of the following is the best description of sustainable farming?

   a   The use of no chemicals by the grower for any purpose.

   b   Maximising yields by the use of modern technology.

   c   Using processes that allow the use of the same resources for future generations.

   d   Only using naturally occurring products when farming an area.

   e   Using traditional farming techniques.

2   Crop rotation has a number of beneficial impacts which help the development of sustainable methods. Explain how this technique helps in each of these situations.

Issue	Explanation
Pest and disease control	
Soil cultivation	
Fertiliser use	
Improved human diet	
Reduction in crop over-supply	

3 Describe **three** ways in which water can be used to irrigate crops more efficiently.

....

....

....

....

....

....

4 It is often recommended that, whereas all fertilisers carry risks of environmental damage if used incorrectly, the use of organic fertilisers is the more sustainable option. Give **three** reasons why this is the case.

....

....

....

....

....

....

5 Genetic modification is considered by many to be bad for the environment. Present an argument to support the case that this technology can help provide a sustainable approach to agriculture.

....

....

....

....

....

....

....

....

....

Water and its management

This chapter covers the following topics:

- the distribution of water on Earth
- the water cycle
- why humans need water
- the main sources of fresh water for human use
- availability of safe drinking water around the world
- multipurpose dam projects
- water-related diseases
- disposing of human waste safely and delivering potable water to people
- pollution of water by industry
- acid rain
- eutrophication.

Exercise 4.1   The distribution of water on Earth

> This exercise will give you practice at calculating percentages and deriving figures from percentages in the context of how water is distributed on Earth.

1   The Earth has 1.4 billion km³ of water. Only 3% is fresh water, the rest is saline. Calculate how many cubic kilometres of the Earth's water is saline.

....

....

....

....

2   There are about 13 000 km³ of water, in the form of water vapour, in the Earth's atmosphere. Calculate the percentage of the Earth's water this represents, using the figure for the total water on Earth from question 1.

....

....

....

....

Exercise 4.2 The water cycle

This exercise will give you practice in describing and interpreting the water cycle and help you to become more familiar with all the terms that describe the various processes.

1   Use these words to fill in the gaps in the sentences below.

evaporation   surface run-off   infiltration   intercepted

Some rainfall does not reach the ground because it is .... by trees and plants.

Some rainfall flows over the surface and ends up in streams and rivers. This is called

....

Some rainfall re-enters the atmosphere in a process called ....

Some rainfall seeps into the ground, which is called ....

2   Explain how a molecule of water might leave the ocean and then re-enter it one month later. Use the following words in your answer.

plants   roots   precipitation   evaporation   infiltration   condensation

....

....

....

....

....

3   Look at the water cycle diagram.

    a Write the correct names next to the arrows to show processes in the water cycle.

    b Add labels and arrows to the diagram to show:

    run-off   interception   condensation

4 What is groundwater?

....

....

....

5 Explain the difference between through-flow and ground-water flow.

....

....

....

....

....

6 Explain how run-off might change if an area of forested land was developed to create a hotel complex.

....

....

....

Exercise 4.3 Why humans need water

This exercise will help you to learn the reasons why water is so important to both traditional rural and modern societies. You will also have some practice in simple calculations and the production of pie charts.

1 State **one** industrial and **one** domestic use of water.

....

....

2 'Water for agricultural use does not need to be potable.'

Explain whether or not you agree with this statement.

....

....

3 The table shows the water usage in India, by percent for each category.

irrigation	68
domestic	7
industry	

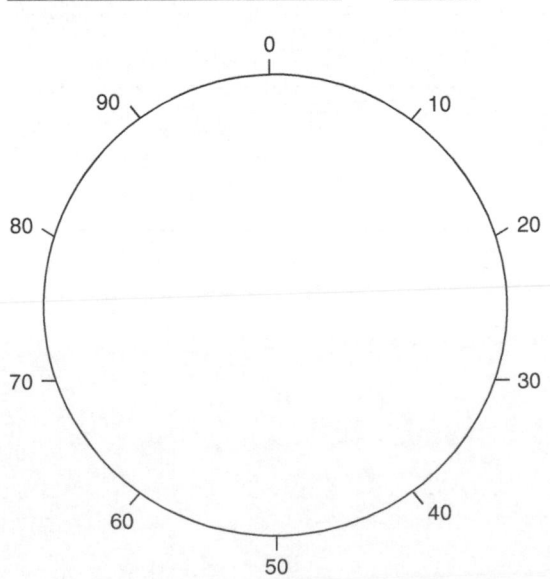

Complete the table, pie chart and key.

Exercise 4.4 The main sources of fresh water for human use

This exercise will allow you to review your understanding of where humans get their water from. This will be in terms of both a modern society and a traditional rural one.

1 Suggest a source of water for a poor country with very low rainfall.

....

....

2 Give **one** difference between the water in a bank-side reservoir and that in a service reservoir.

....

....

3 Name **two** rock types that could accumulate water in an aquifer.

....

....

4 Give the name of an underground water store which does not require a pump to extract the water.

....

....

5 Distinguish between distillation and desalination.

....

....

....

....

6 An environmental scientist thinks that reverse osmosis is a more sustainable method of obtaining drinking water from the sea than distillation. Explain how far you agree or disagree with this opinion.

....

....

....

....

....

....

....

Exercise 4.5 Availability of safe drinking water around the world

This exercise will help you to understand the word 'potable' and the importance of a supply of potable water to people. It will also check your knowledge of the different forms of water scarcity and the principles of how water can be made safer. Finally, it will consider how successful drives to improve water safety have been.

1 Give **two** reasons why a country with plentiful rainfall may still be considered to have problems supplying enough safe water to its people.

....

....

....

....

2 Distinguish between physical and economic water scarcity.

....

....

....

3 Improved sanitation and water treatment are both strategies used to ensure potable water is supplied to people.

Explain the differences between sanitation and water treatment.

....

....

....

....

4 In 2000, 77% of the world's population had access to safe water. In 2016, the figure had risen to 91%.

Describe and explain the change in the percentage without access to safe water between 2000 and 2016.

....

....

....

....

....

Exercise 4.6 Multipurpose dam projects

> **This exercise will allow you to evaluate dam projects and consider some of the factors to be borne in mind when planning them.**

1 'It can only be beneficial to build a dam.' How far do you agree with this statement?

....

....

....

....

....

....

2 The map shows the location of a large dam. Suggest why this is a good site for a dam.

....

....

....

....

....

....

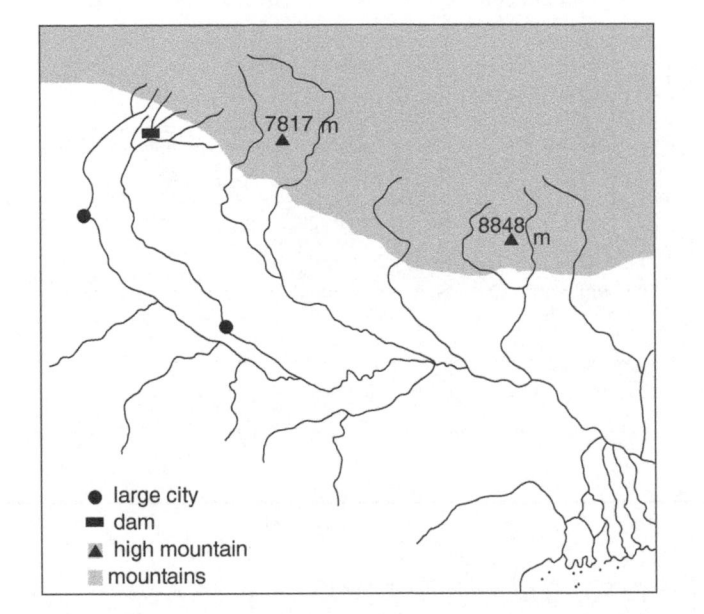

3 Suggest **three** purposes of a multipurpose dam project.

....

....

....

....

....

....

Exercise 4.7 Water-related diseases

> This exercise will help you to check your understanding of how malaria is transmitted. Understanding how malaria is transmitted helps you to understand how the disease can be controlled and eradicated. Remember that malaria is not a bacterial disease.
>
> The exercise also looks at the water-borne bacterial diseases cholera and typhoid.

For successful cultivation of rice, the fields need to be flooded with water. Malaria is common in areas where rice is grown.

1 Name the vector that carries malaria.

   ....

2 Explain why malaria is common in areas where rice is grown.

   ....

   ....

   ....

3 Villagers were concerned about the many deaths due to malaria. They decided to try and reduce the death rate. Some ideas suggested were:

   a spraying inside their huts with insecticide

   b purchasing nets to sleep under at night

   c covering bodies of water with oil.

   For each idea, suggest how it would help to reduce the death rate from malaria.

   ....

   ....

   ....

   ....

   ....

   ....

4 Suggest **one** other way by which the death rate from malaria could be reduced.

....

....

....

5 A sign next to a water supply says 'This is not drinking water'. Suggest one reason why it might say this.

6 Which of the following water-borne diseases can be controlled by boiling water before drinking it? Circle the answer.

cholera   malaria   typhoid

Exercise 4.8 Disposing of human waste safely and delivering potable water to people

> With over 7000 million people on the planet, disposing safely of human waste is a big problem. This exercise will help you to revise how this is done and how potable water can be delivered to people for drinking.

1 The average person produces 30 kilograms (dry weight) of sewage per year. If this sewage comes into contact with drinking water it can affect human health.

Explain why it is important for human health to keep sewage and drinking water separate.

....

....

....

2 Use these words to complete this paragraph about sewage treatment. (You may need to use some words more than once.)

chlorine   bacteria   organic   treatment   larger   oxygen

Sewage is treated to reduce the amount of .... material.

If this is not done before the sewage is sent to a river, then .... will break

it down, producing a biological .... demand. To make river water potable, it is passed through a water .... plant. The water is filtered to

remove .... particles. It is disinfected with .... to

kill ....

Exercise 4.9 Pollution of water by industry

> Toxic compounds from industrial processes include heavy metals, which can build up along food
> chains by bioaccumulation. The following questions help you to explore such situations.

A new chemical factory was set up on a river. Several years later it was noticed that fish were dying in the river
downstream of the factory. People in a local village relied on the river for fish. The water was tested and found to
contain mercury.

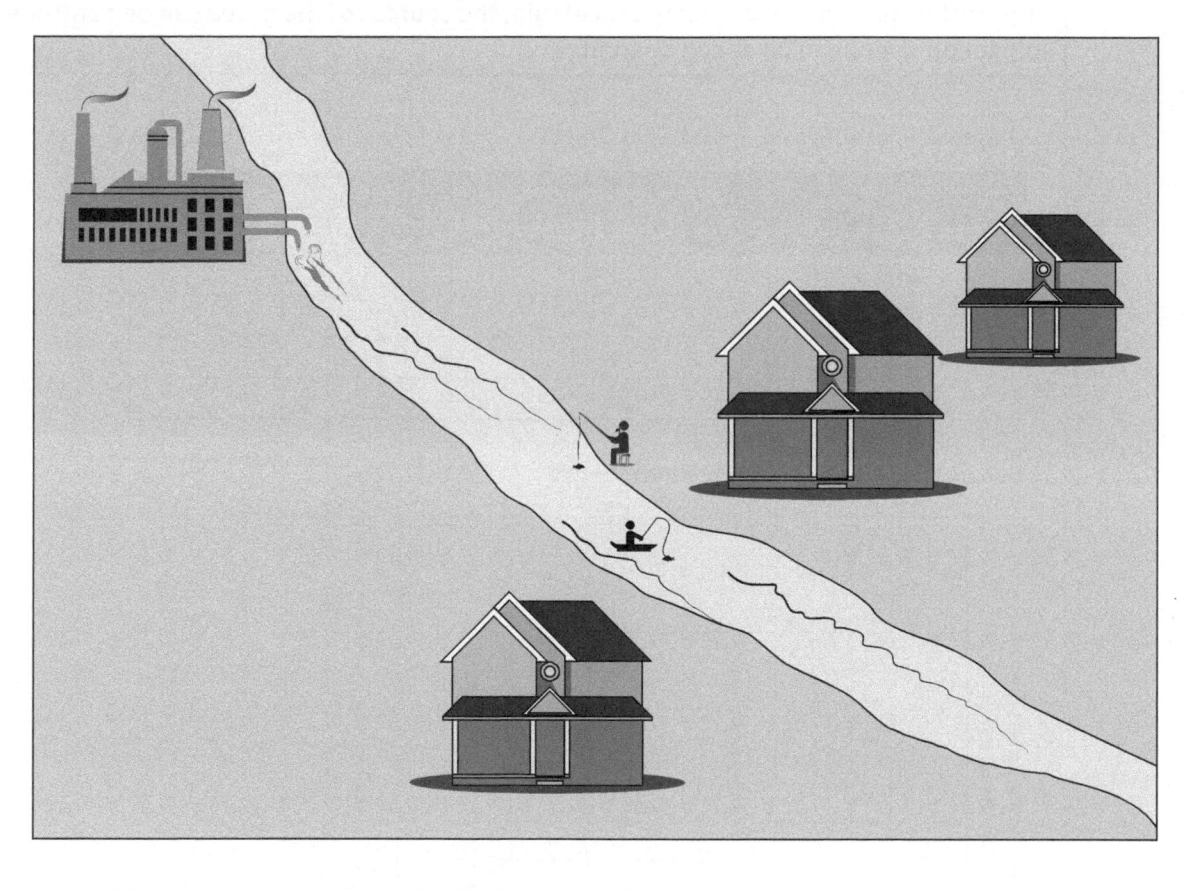

1 Explain why it took several years for the fish to start dying.

....

....

....

2 Suggest the risks to human health caused by this factory.

....

....

....

Exercise 4.10 Acid rain

Acid rain is an important topic in environmental management. The gases involved start off in the atmosphere and become 'acid rain' when they dissolve in rain. The problems then result when this rain comes down to rivers and lakes and also when the rain infiltrates through soil. This exercise covers the production of acid rain gases and their impact on water bodies. There are two approaches to reduce the effects of acid rain: the sources of the gases can be controlled, and the impact on rivers and lakes can be treated.

1 The table shows industrial and domestic emissions of sulfur dioxide in a developed country over a four-year period.

Year	Sulfur dioxide emissions / million tonnes per year	
	Industrial	Domestic
2010	2220	360
2011	2140	340
2012	1990	340
2013	1850	360

Plot a suitable graph of these data on the grid provided.

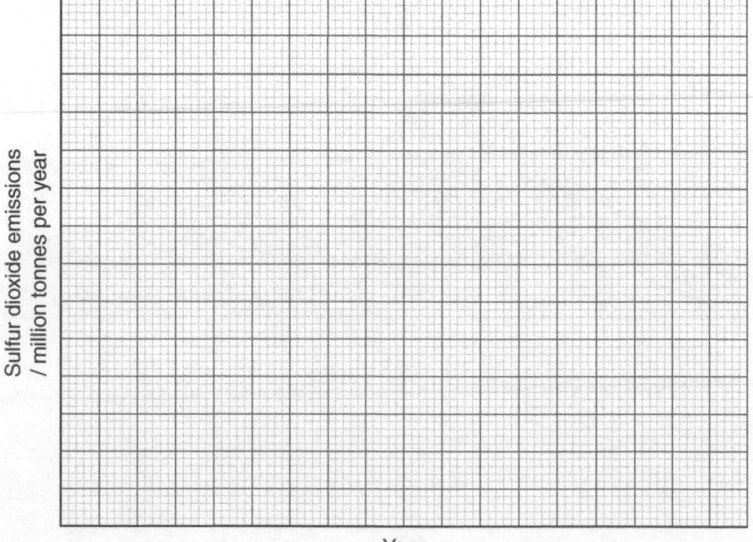

Year

2 The wealth of the country increased over the 4 years.

Give reasons for the difference in the trends shown in industrial and domestic emissions.

....

....

....

....

....

....

3 Explain how acid rain is formed from sulfur dioxide and at least one other atmospheric pollutant.

....

....

....

....

The maps show exports and imports of sulfur dioxide and NO_x to and from Sweden.

4 Calculate the amount of total sulfur dioxide imported into Sweden from other countries.

....

5 How many countries are known to export both NO_x and sulfur dioxide to Sweden?

....

6 Of the sulfur dioxide that Sweden produces, 11 million tonnes is not exported.

Calculate this as a percentage of the total amount of sulfur dioxide that affects Sweden every year.

.... %

7 Using the maps and the calculations, explain why acid rain is considered to be an international problem.

....

....

....

....

....

....

Exercise 4.11 Eutrophication

> Eutrophication is a sequence of events, which starts with an input into a water system and ends with a lack of oxygen. If the input is due to fertiliser use on farms, then this will increase plant growth. If the input is organic matter in sewage, then decomposition by bacteria will be involved straight away. It is important to remember that oxygen is used in respiration and carbon dioxide is used in photosynthesis with oxygen being produced. Also, the bacteria that decompose dead plant material use oxygen for respiration.

1 Eutrophication of rivers can be caused by chemicals coming from farms and houses. This can lead to the death of fish. You will see from the diagram that as X and Y increase, Z decreases.

Suggest the names of the chemicals/substances involved at X, Y and Z.

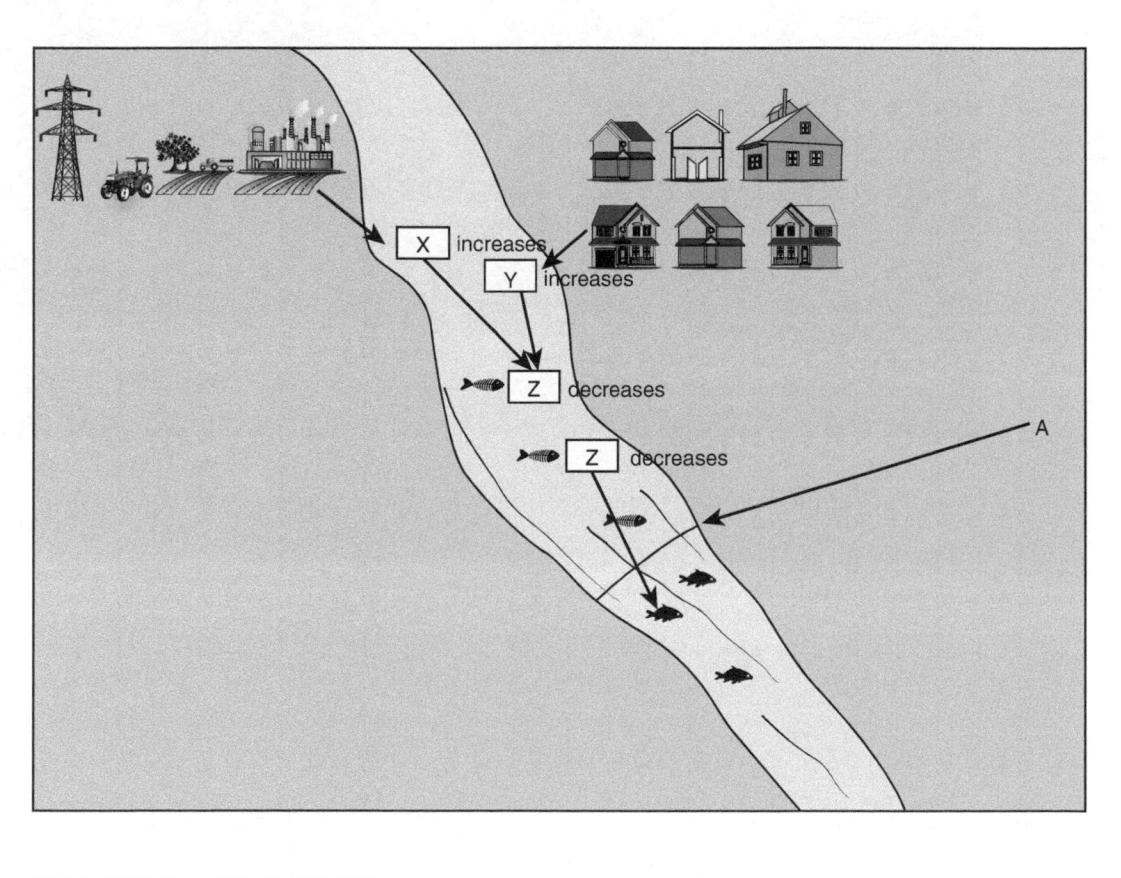

....

....

....

....

2 A weir was built at position A on the previous diagram.

Using the information in the diagram and the photograph, explain the effect of this weir on the river.

....

....

....

3 A student used a newspaper account of the death of fish in a local lake to draw a eutrophication flow chart for a school poster project.

The chart is shown below.

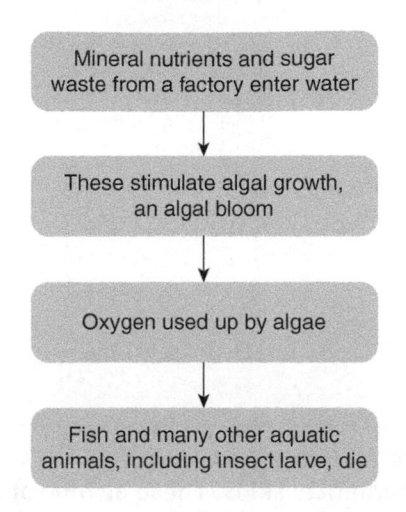

Mineral nutrients and sugar waste from a factory enter water

These stimulate algal growth, an algal bloom

Oxygen used up by algae

Fish and many other aquatic animals, including insect larve, die

Explain the errors in the chart and then write a correct account of eutrophication.

....

....

....

....

....

....

4 It was noticed that the community of animals and plants in two small lakes, which were quite close together, were very different. It was suggested that this might be due to differences in the nutrients in the lake. Plan an investigation that could be used to compare the effects of enrichment with nitrate on these two different bodies of water.

....

....

....

....

....

....

Oceans and fisheries

This chapter covers the following topics:

- the resource potential of the oceans
- world fisheries
- exploitation of the oceans: impact on fisheries
- strategies for managing the harvesting of marine species.

Exercise 5.1 The resource potential of the oceans

This exercise will help with your understanding of what humans can get from the oceans. You will also have the chance to practise some simple mathematical skills. These include percentages, proportions and using maths to compare costs and benefits.

1   List **three** products and **two** services which the sea can provide.

....

....

....

....

2   By far the largest proportion of the water on Earth is in the oceans. Water is one of the main requirements of life, but it is often in short supply for humans. Explain why humans cannot use seawater for drinking.

....

....

....

....

3 List the characteristics of goods which are best transported by sea compared with those best transported by air.

....

....

....

....

....

4 Total world registered tonnage of merchant ships is 1034.3 million. Japan has 17.8 million tonnes of registered merchant ships. Calculate the percentage that the Japanese merchant fleet represents of the world total.

....

71

5 Read this extract about tourism and the oceans.

> The seaside has been a major tourist attraction for centuries. Over 2000 years ago, the Romans enjoyed sea, sun and sand in Baiae when in Rome, and on Mersae when in England. Today, with cheap air travel, people in the more economically developed countries (MEDCs) of the world are attracted to marine sites of great natural beauty, especially coral reefs. Visitors in their hundreds of thousands arrive every year round the Caribbean, the Red Sea, the Indian Ocean (for example the Maldives) and on the Great Barrier Reef of Australia. Diving, snorkeling, windsurfing and jet skiing are just some of the activities for the more adventurous, but many are content simply to sunbathe on the beach. Away from the shore, deep-sea fishing is a very popular pastime. In addition, there is big business in boat trips to view the creatures of the sea, especially whales and dolphins. Whale watching began in the mid-1950s on the coast of California as a chance event. It was not until whaling was banned in the early 1980s that people began to see watching whales as an economic alternative to killing them.

Use this information to describe the distribution of coral reefs.

....

....

....

....

....

6   The largest power plant in the world is that at the Three Gorges Dam in China. Its capacity is 22 500 MW. At the same time of writing, the biggest tidal power station in the world is the Sihwa Lake Tidal Power Station in South Korea, with a capacity of 254 MW. Calculate how many times bigger the capacity of Three Gorges Dam is than Sihwa Lake Tidal Power Station.

....

7   Sihwa Lake Tidal Power Station cost US$293 million to build. The Three Gorges Dam project cost US$37 billion. Compare the costs per megawatt of these two power generation strategies.

....

....

....

....

....

....

....

Exercise 5.2 World fisheries

This exercise will help with your understanding of the importance of fish, both to the human diet and to the economy of many regions of the world. You will also be able to revise why fisheries are found where they are. You can try out your graph plotting skills and how to use evidence to support a theory.

1 Which food group includes fish?

....

2 Explain why the largest fish populations are found in shallow water where there is an upwelling.

....

....

....

....

....

....

....

3 Only 0.03% or so of the atmosphere is made up of carbon dioxide. It is much more abundant in the sea. Explain why.

....

....

....

4 In which of the following areas are large fish populations most likely to be found? Give one answer.

A deep ocean

B abyssal plain

C continental shelf

D continental slope

....

5 The top map, below, shows the continental shelves surrounding the world's continents. The bottom map shows the major warm and cold ocean currents. Using the diagrams and your own knowledge, suggest why there is no large fishery to the east or west of India.

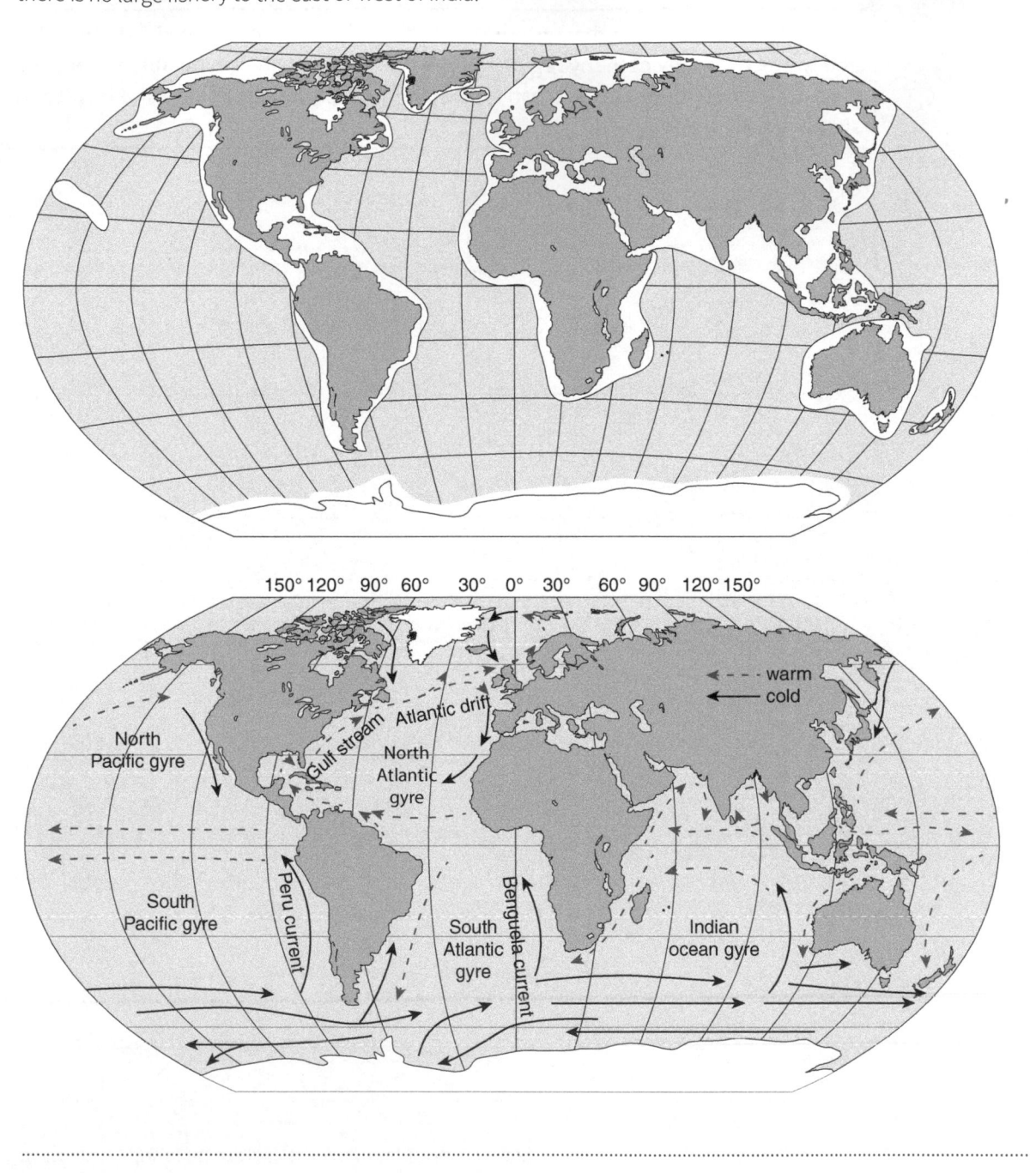

....

....

....

....

6 The table shows the fish catch off the coast of Peru between 1990 and 2003.

Year	Catch / 1000 tonnes
1990	3900
1991	4000
1992	6100
1993	8500
1994	12500
1995	8600
1996	8700
1997	7500
1998	1800
1999	8600
2000	11300
2001	7200
2002	9800
2003	6100

Draw a bar chart using the data from the table. Don't forget to label your axes appropriately.

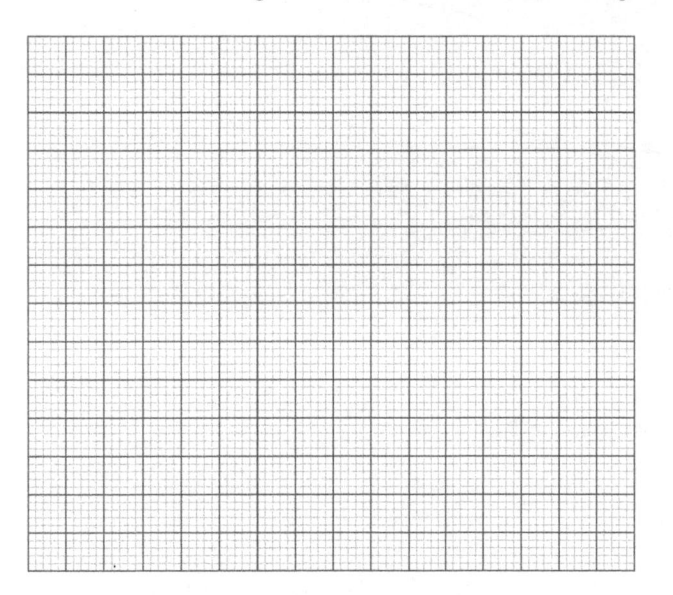

7 Use the data shown in question 6. Suggest **two** possible explanations for the catch in 1998 and explain which you think is the most likely.

....

....

Exercise 5.3 Exploitation of the oceans: impact on fisheries

This exercise will help with your understanding of how fish are exploited. It will also give you some further maths skill practice.

1 State **three** types of bycatch.

....

....

....

2 Look at the diagram. Use the information to calculate the percentage decrease in the mass of cod between the 1930s and the 2000s.

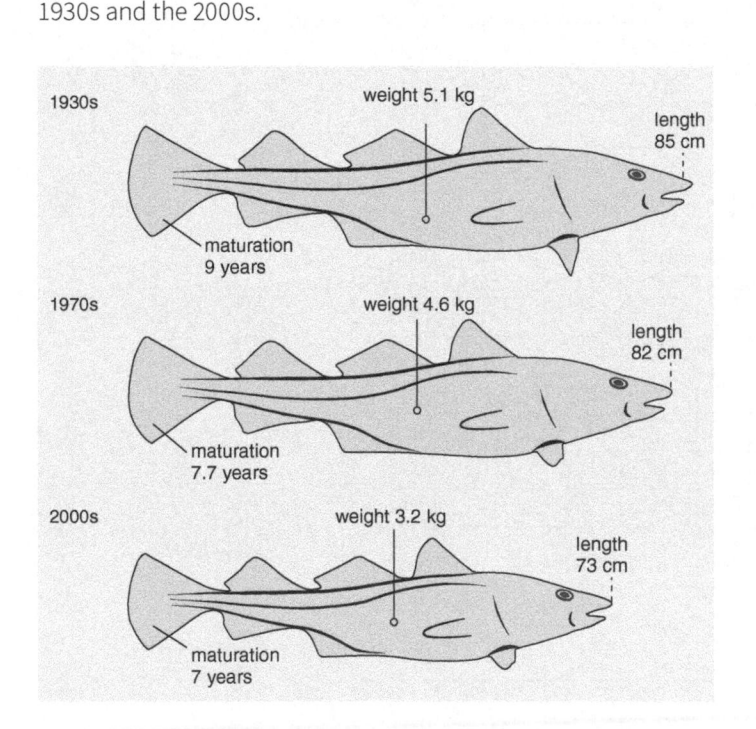

....

....

....

3 List **three** reasons for overfishing.

....

....

....

....

....

4 Give **one** reason why it is difficult to farm marine fish as food.

....

....

....

Exercise 5.4 Strategies for managing the harvesting of marine species

This exercise will help with your understanding of how we manage fisheries sustainably.

1 One simple way of reducing the effect of massive nets on fish populations is to ban them. However, this is not always easy to enforce. A more subtle way of reducing the effect of these nets is to think about mesh size rather than net size. In one such strategy, an agreement was reached to make the closed end of a net have a minimum of 40 mm square mesh. Explain how this strategy can help in the conservation of fish stocks.

....

....

....

....

....

....

2 Explain how the strategy described in question 1 can be thought of as an example of sustainability.

....

....

....

3 Explain what is meant by the word quota in the context of fisheries and how a quota system may be enforced.

....

....

....

....

....

....

4 Complete the following passage.

Governments try to protect fish stocks by setting limits on the numbers caught, called a

.... Another strategy involves closing the fishery down for part of the year.

This is referred to as a .... Finally,

fishermen can be prevented from operating in certain areas, called protected areas, which are often the main

.... area for the fish.

5 Despite all the strategies available to governments and others, it is very difficult to protect fish stocks effectively. Explain why.

....

....

....

....

....

....

6 The sea cucumber, *Isostichopus fuscus*, is a slow-moving animal, which lives on the seabed and feeds on small organic particles. In 1991, people began fishing for the sea cucumber around the Galapagos Islands in the Pacific Ocean to the west of Ecuador. However, the fishery had many problems and the Ecuadorian government banned it in 1992. Some fishing happened in 1994, but the ban was re-imposed until 1999. When the fishery was reopened in 1999, the government required surveys to be carried out every year, both before and after the fishing season. The data collected was the number of individual sea cucumbers in a defined area.

a Write a plan for a survey, which could be carried out every year before the fishing season and again after the fishing season.

....

....

....

....

....

....

....

....

The results of these surveys, between 1999 and 2005, are shown in the graph.

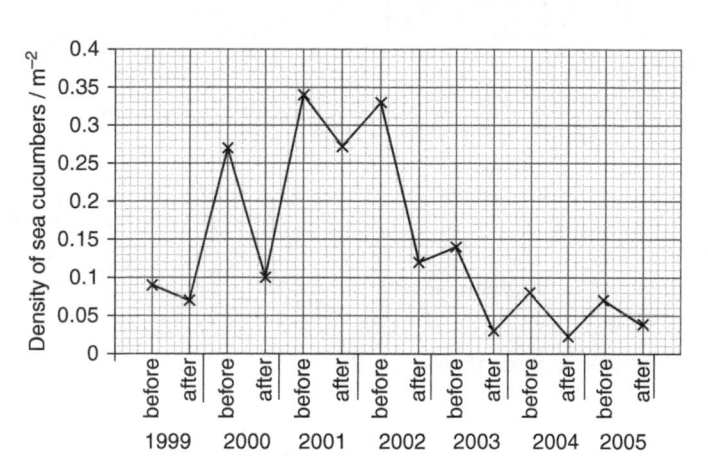

b In what year did the recorded density of sea cucumbers decrease the most? Calculate the size of the decrease.

....

....

c Describe and explain the patterns shown by these results.

....

....

....

d Do you think there are any trends in the data? Explain your answer.

....

....

....

e In order to take pressure off the natural population, investigations are being carried out into the possibility of culturing sea cucumbers.

In one experiment, sea cucumbers were kept in tanks of seawater and fed with different food. Some young sea cucumbers weighing 0.8 g were placed into two separate tanks which had seawater flowing through them. The sea cucumbers were fed with different diets in the two tanks. In tank A they were fed chicken manure and in tank B they were fed with shrimp starter as food. The sea cucumbers were weighed every 15 days for 45 days. The arrangement of the tanks is shown in the diagram.

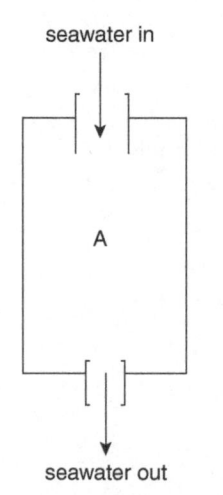
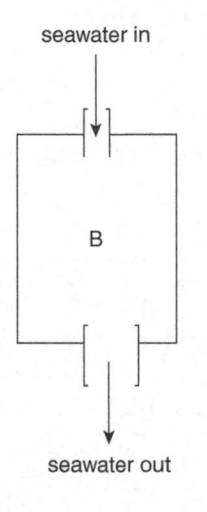

Using all the information and the diagram, together with your own knowledge, identify some limitations in this experiment. Suggest how it could be improved.

....

....

....

....

....

....

....

....

....

The results from the experiment described are shown in the graph.

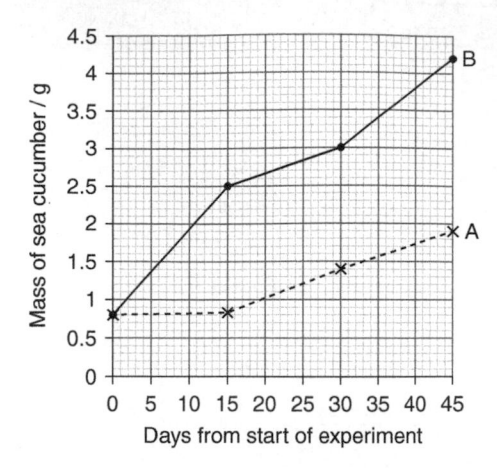

f   Compare the trend in the data for the two graphs.

....

....

....

....

....

....

Managing natural hazards

This chapter covers the following topics:

- definitions
- comparing natural hazards, focusing on volcanoes
- flooding and management strategies
- the impacts of drought.
- the impacts of tropical cyclones
- the review of natural hazards

Exercise 6.1 Definitions

> In this exercise you will revise some definitions that you will need to understand the material in this chapter.

For each question, write the correct word in the space to complete the definition. Choose from these words.

| oceanic | destructive | lithosphere | basaltic | fold mountains |

composite   oceanic trench

1 **Tectonic plate**   A piece of .... which moves slowly on the asthenosphere.

2 **Plate boundary**   Where two or more plates meet. There are three main types of plate boundary: constructive,

.... and conservative.

3 .... are created where two or more tectonic plates are pushed together. Rocks are compressed and folded upwards.

4 **Shield volcano**   A broad volcano built up from the repeated eruption of .... lava.

5 **Subduction zone**   A zone where the .... plate is deflected down into the mantle. At the surface, the subduction zone coincides with ocean trenches.

6 .... A depression of the ocean floor which runs parallel to a destructive plate boundary.

7 .... **volcano**   Conical in shape and built up by many layers of lava and ash.

Exercise 6.2 Comparing natural hazards, focusing on volcanoes

This exercise will help you to improve your knowledge of natural hazards and volcanoes. It will give you practice in calculating percentages and drawing bar graphs and pie charts.

It is estimated that 836 870 people died in natural disasters between 2005 and 2015.

1   Complete the table below by calculating the percentage of deaths caused by the natural disasters listed.

Natural disaster type	Number of deaths 2005 to 2015 in natural disasters	% of deaths from selected natural disasters 2005 to 2015
Earthquakes	411 090	
Volcanoes	463	
Tropical cyclones	170 251	
Floods	60 855	
Droughts	20 421	

2   Plot the % of each natural disaster type as a bar graph on the grid below. Choose appropriate scales. Label the axes. Plot the points accurately and complete a key.

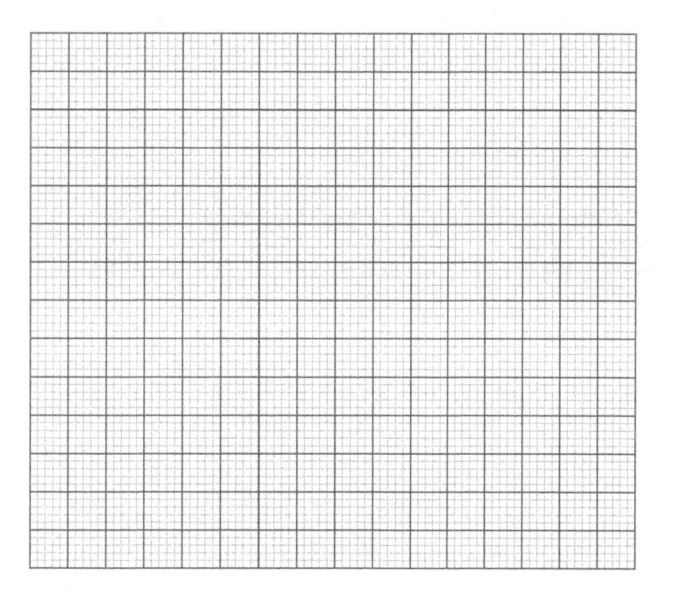

3   Why do you think fewer people are killed by volcanoes than by earthquakes?

....

....

....

....

....

4   In the space below, draw an annotated diagram to show the cross-section through a constructive plate boundary. Label the following features on your diagram and give it a title.

North American Plate (oceanic)   Eurasian Plate (oceanic)   direction of plate movement

convection current   mid ocean ridge   shield volcano   ocean   mantle

5   In the space below, draw an annotated diagram to show the cross-section through a destructive plate boundary. Label the following features on your diagram and give it a title.

Nazca Plate (oceanic plate)   South American Plate (continental plate)   direction of plate movement

mantle   ocean trench   subduction zone   rising magma   composite volcano

fold mountains (Andes)

6 The diagram shows features of a volcano. Complete the labels at A, B, C and D to show the features of a volcano.

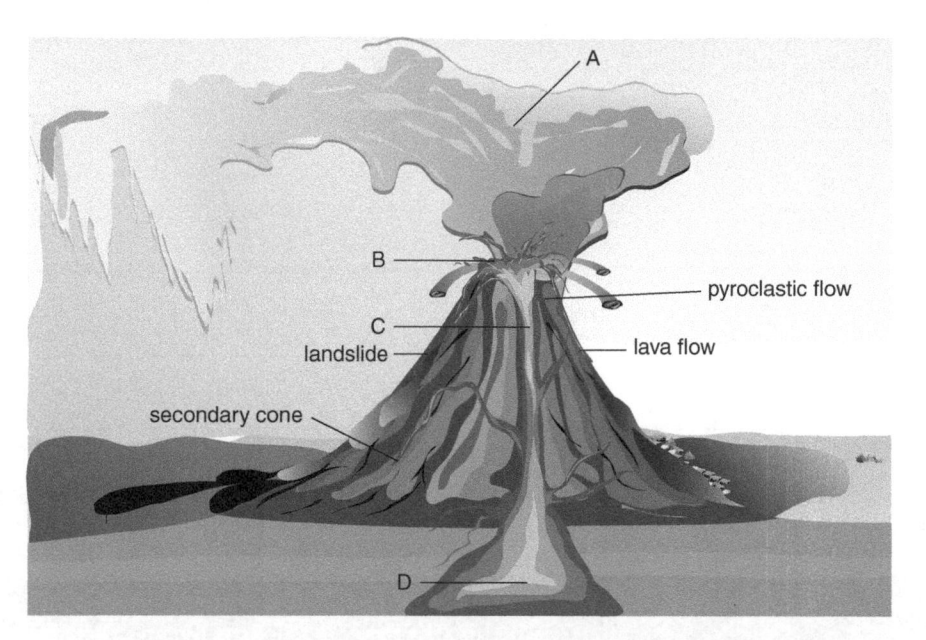

7 The table shows the estimated percentage of deaths by volcanic activity between 1915 and 2015 by region.

Region	% of deaths caused by volcanic activity 1915 to 2015
Africa	5
North America	1
Central and South America	58
Asia	29
Europe	0.5
Oceania	6.5

Use the data in the table and the key to draw a pie chart to display the data.

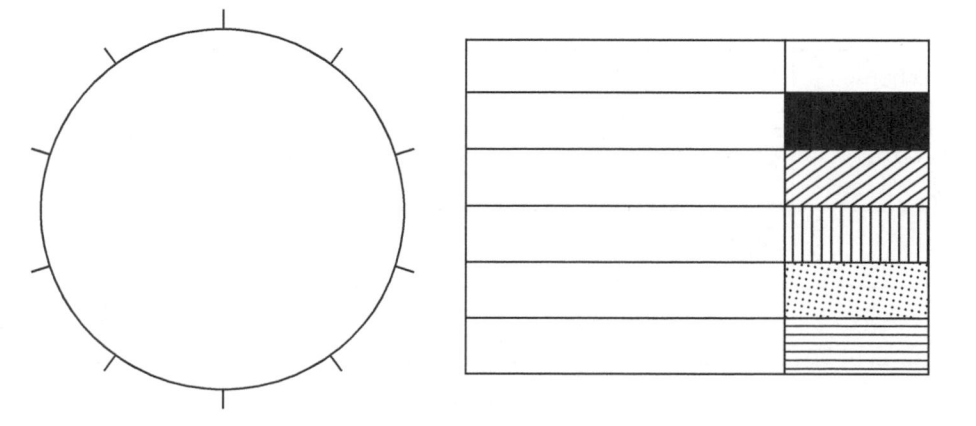

8 In which regions of the world do most deaths from volcanic activity occur? Suggest **three** reasons why this is the case.

....

....

....

....

....

....

9 The table below shows the primary causes of death by the ten volcanoes that killed the most people between 1915 and 2015.

Volcano	Country	Year	Number of deaths by pyroclastic flow	Number of deaths by lahars	Number of deaths by ashfall	Number of deaths by gas
Kelut	Indonesia	1919		5110		
Merapi	Indonesia	1930	1369			
Rabaul Caldera	Papua New Guinea	1937	507			
Lamington	Papua New Guinea	1951	2942			
Hibok-Hibok	Philippines	1951	500			
Agung	Indonesia	1963	1148			
El Chichon	Mexico	1982	2000			
Nevado del Ruiz	Colombia	1985		23 000		
Lake Nyos	Cameroon	1986				1700
Mt Pinatubo	Philippines	1991			300	

Present the data showing the primary cause of death by the volcanoes in rank order of cause of death, from the highest to lowest, by completing the table below.

Primary cause of death	Number of deaths

10 Describe **four** major problems that survivors of a volcanic eruption might face.

....

....

....

....

....

....

....

....

11 Complete the spider diagram below to show four different strategies that can be used to prevent loss of life from a volcanic eruption.

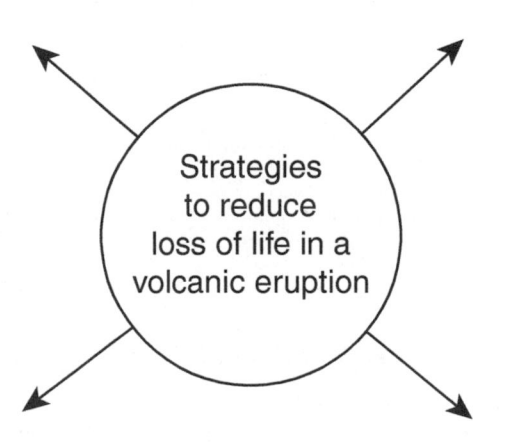

Strategies to reduce loss of life in a volcanic eruption

12 Study the table below which shows information about two volcanoes.

Year of eruption	Name of volcano	Location	Level of development	Number of people evacuated from their homes
2014	Bardarbunga	Iceland	More Economically Developed Country	300
2014	Sinabung	Indonesia	Less Economically Developed Country	20 000

Suggest reasons why there was a difference in the number of people evacuated from their homes.

....

....

....

....

....

....

....

13 Why are people still prepared to live near volcanoes?

....

....

....

....

....

....

....

Exercise 6.3 Flooding and management strategies

This exercise will check your knowledge of flooding. It will also give you a chance to practise your evaluation skills in relation to strategies for managing floods.

For questions 1 to 5, write the correct word in the space to complete the definition. Choose from these words.

interception   infiltration   impermeable   floodplain   afforestation

1 .... Low-lying land next to a river channel that gets flooded when a river overflows.

2 .... Doesn't allow water to pass through easily.

3 .... Planting trees in areas that have never been forested.

4 .... Water passing from the surface into the soil.

5 .... Rain is temporarily stored on vegetation.

6 What is meant by river flooding?

....

....

....

....

7 There are many reasons why a river floods. Draw a line to link each cause of flooding to the correct explanation.

deforestation	The infiltration capacity is quickly exceeded and overland flow takes place.
previous weather	Concrete and tarmac are impermeable and lead to more overland flow.
rock type	If trees are removed there is less interception and infiltration.
relief	Impermeable rock leads to greater overland flow.
heavy rainfall	The more saturated the soil the less infiltration can take place.
urbanisation	Steeper gradients lead to faster overland flow.

Read the newspaper extracts below which refer to two flood events which happened in 2015. The first flood occurred in the south of France (an MEDC), the second was in Malawi, an LEDC, in Africa.

Storms hit French Rivieria

The River Brague near Antibes, which lies between Nice and Cannes, burst its banks killing 19 people. Nice normally receives an average of 733 mm of rainfall a year, but it was reported that 10% of this figure fell in just two days. Cars were washed into the sea and buildings were knee deep in muddy water. 27 000 homes lost electricity for a few hours. Those affected will be able to claim damages and financial support from the French government.

Worst floods in living memory hit Malawi

Flooding has killed 276 people and left 30 000 homeless. Livestock and possessions have been swept away. 64 000 hectares of land has been damaged: a devastating amount as most Malawians survive by subsistence farming. The concern of relief organisations is that water-borne diseases will break out in the over-crowded evacuation camps. Very heavy rains have been blamed but experts also say that deforestation has been taking place at a rapid pace.

8 What was the common cause of flooding in these two events?

....

....

9 How can deforestation in Malawi contribute to the flooding?

....

....

....

....

10 Compare the number of people who died in these two flooding events.

....

....

11 Describe how the effects of the flooding in a more economically developed country such as France are different from the effects in a less economically developed country such as Malawi.

....

....

....

....

....

....

12 State **one** positive impact of flooding.

....

....

13 Write the correct word in the spaces from the list to complete the passage.

natural   control   structures   land use zoning   dams   flood walls   afforestation

Hard engineering strategies are .... that are constructed to try to

.... the river. Examples of hard engineering are

.... and .... Soft engineering works with

the river and its drainage basin and uses .... processes. Examples include

.... and ....

14 Are hard engineering projects an appropriate strategy to reduce floods in a less economically developed country? Explain your answer.

....

....

....

....

....

....

....

....

Exercise 6.4 The impacts of drought

This exercise will check your knowledge of droughts, as well as giving you more practice in drawing and analysing climate graphs.

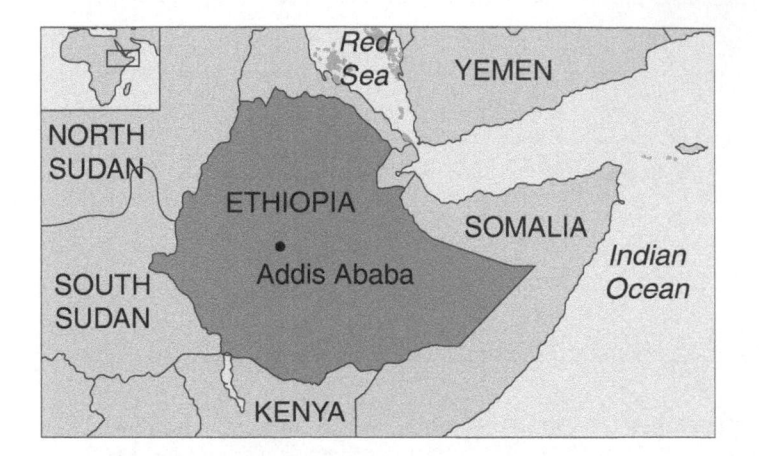

1   Ethiopia is a country in East Africa. On the graph paper below, plot the mean monthly temperatures using a line graph, and the mean monthly rainfall using a bar graph, for Addis Ababa, the capital city of Ethiopia. Remember to label the axes.

	J	F	M	A	M	J	J	A	S	O	N	D
Mean monthly temperature (°C)	16	16	17	17	18	17	15	15	16	15	15	15
Mean monthly precipitation (mm)	20	32	54	56	96	112	245	270	117	40	10	13

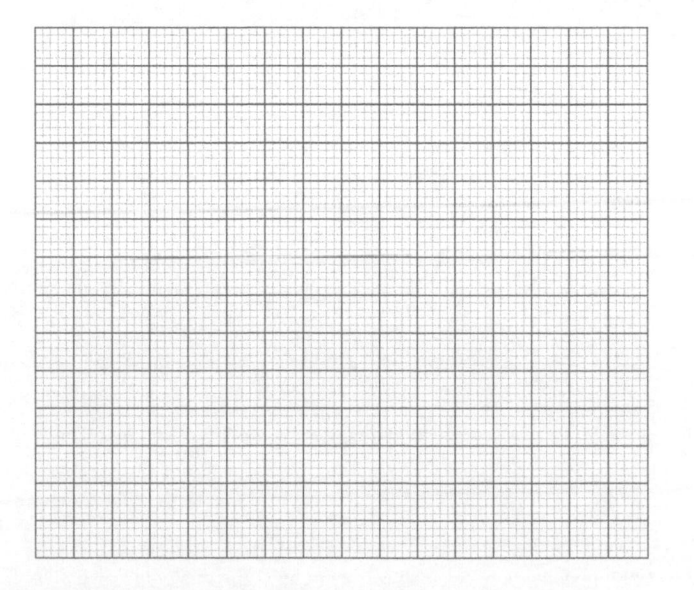

2   What is the total mean annual rainfall? Circle **one** answer.

1006 mm   1065 mm   165 mm   1650 mm

3   What is the annual range of temperature for Addis Ababa?

....

4   Look again at the climate graph of Addis Ababa you have drawn. In which months of the year do you think
farmers will experience difficulties in growing crops and raising livestock? Explain your answer.

....

....

....

....

5   Read the two extracts below about the causes and effects of drought in two contrasting areas of the world.
Extract A is about Ethiopia and extract B is about California in the United States.

Extract A

In 2015, Ethiopia faced its worst drought in 50 years due to the failure of the spring rains,
compounded by El Nino conditions that reduced the summer rains. Central and eastern parts of
the country received 25% less rainfall than normal. Charity organisations claimed that 10% of the
population would need emergency food assistance in 2016 if acute malnutrition and fatalities were
to be avoided. There have been severe crop and livestock losses. Farmers are selling off remaining
livestock as they can no longer feed them and moving to urban areas.

Extract B

2011 to 2015 were the driest years in California since records began in 1895. Drought conditions
were made worse by higher temperatures resulting in less snow and hence less snowmelt in the
Sierra Nevada mountains. Farming in the State depends on irrigation, but lakes and reservoirs
are drying up, resulting in crop losses worth over 2.2 billion $US. Over 17,000 have lost their jobs
in this sector. Output from hydroelectric power plants has been reduced, golf courses have closed
and homes and businesses have water restrictions. More desalination plants are to be built.

a   Compare and contrast the causes of drought in Ethiopia and California.

....

....

....

....

....

....

b How do the two extracts show that it is often countries at the lowest level of economic development that suffer most from natural hazards?

....

....

....

....

6 Suggest **two** sustainable methods of reducing the impact of droughts.

....

....

....

....

....

....

Exercise 6.5 The impacts of tropical cyclones

> This exercise will check your knowledge of tropical cyclones, as well as giving you more practice in analysing data.

1 Using the list below, write the correct answer in the spaces to complete the passage.

| hurricanes | 87 | 5° to 30° | clockwise | 13 | low | 27 | eyewall | counter-clockwise |

| 119 | high | eye | 0° to 15° | typhoons |

Tropical cyclones are .... pressure weather systems that produce winds

of .... km per hour or greater. They develop in the tropics between the

latitudes .... north or south of the equator where the surface ocean

temperatures are greater than ....°C. In the northern hemisphere the

winds rotate around an area of calm called the .... in a direction that is

.... Tropical cyclones are called .... if they

form over the north west Pacific Ocean.

2 Explain the causes of tropical cyclones.

....

....

....

....

....

....

....

....

3 Study the table below which shows the number of typhoons recorded in each month of the year from 1959 to 2015.

Month	Number of typhoons
January	28
February	14
March	26
April	37
May	66
June	106
July	221
August	310
September	280
October	228
November	139
December	69

The month with the lowest number of recorded typhoons was ....

The month with the highest number of recorded typhoons was ....

4 State the percentage of typhoons that were recorded in the month with the highest number.

....

5 Using information in the table, state in which months of the year the typhoon season is.

....

....

6 Study the map below. It shows the path of Typhoon Lando (known internationally as Typhoon Koppu) in October 2015. It was a tropical storm before it became a typhoon. Using the map circle the correct answer in the passage below.

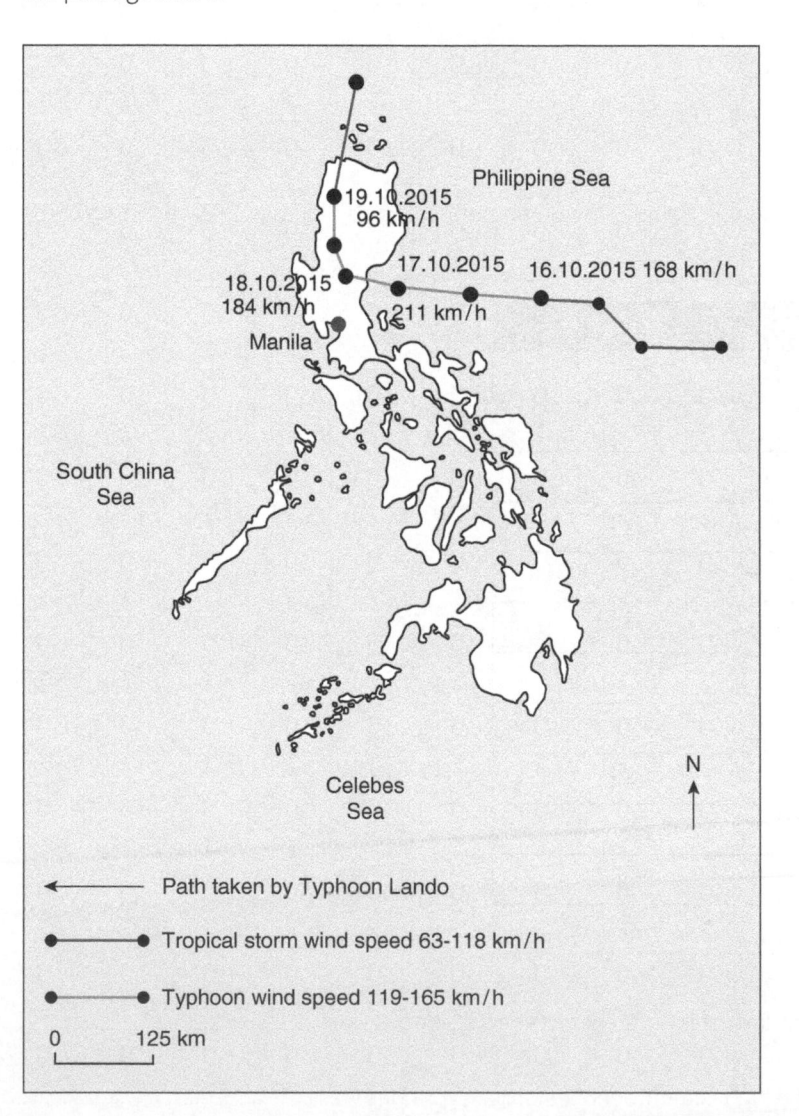

Twenty tropical storms on average hit the Philippine islands each year. Typhoon Lando started as a tropical storm in the **Philippine/Celebes Sea** and moved in an **easterly/westerly** direction. It became a typhoon on the 16th October with wind speeds of **65–118/119–165 km** per hour but passed over the Philippines slowly, north of the city of Manila, across the island of Luzon. Over 300 mm of rain fell across the island over 2 days. The monthly average is usually 182 mm. The typhoon then moved **south/north** and was downgraded to a tropical storm on **19 October/17 October**.

7 Suggest why the authorities in the Philippines were well prepared for Typhoon Lando.

....

....

8 Suggest reasons why people living on low-lying coastal areas, floodplains and mountain slopes on Luzon island were evacuated before Typhoon Lando arrived.

....

....

....

....

9 Study the fact file below showing some of the impacts of Typhoon Lando.

Impacts of Typhoon Lando

58 killed

24 000 people evacuated

90% of rice and corn crop destroyed

Banana and coconut trees blown down

148 roads and 137 bridges unpassable

Electric power cut to 9 million people

Hundreds of villages under 1.5 m of water

Explain **three** immediate problems that the authorities had to manage following Typhoon Lando.

....

....

....

....

....

....

10 A student decided to carry out a survey to investigate the management strategies of Typhoon Lando in Santo Tomas, a town directly hit by the typhoon. Fifty local people were asked to fill in a questionnaire to find out their views.

Suggest why the student used a questionnaire to gain information.

....

....

11 Suggest how the local people could have been selected by the student for the questionnaire.

....

....

....

....

12 The table below shows some of the results from the questionnaire.

Question	Responses to questionnaire		
	yes	no	Do not know
1. Does your community have typhoon management strategies?	47	0	3
2. Did you evacuate before Typhoon Lando arrived?	....	15	0
3. Were you given accurate information regarding evacuation?	34	14	....

Complete the table.

13 Suggest reasons why some people did not evacuate.

....

....

....

....

....

14 Suggest **two** other questions the student could have asked in the questionnaire.

....

....

....

....

15 The diagram below shows some advice given to people by the authorities in the Philippines on how to manage the impacts before and during a typhoon.

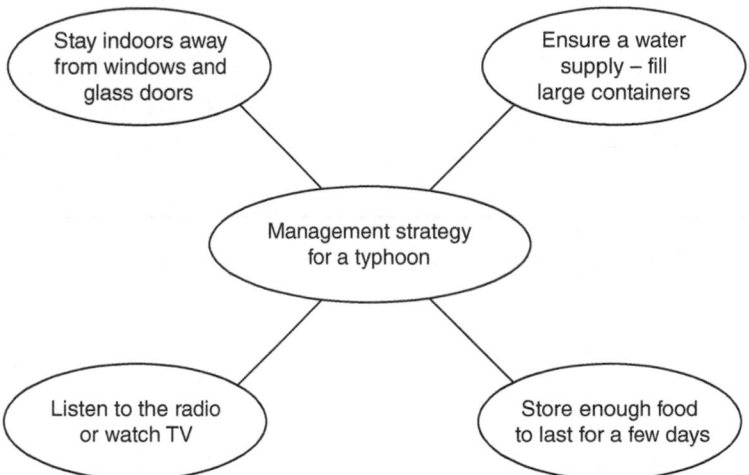

Explain why advice on each of the four management strategies was given to people.

....

....

....

....

....

....

....

....

16 Suggest reasons why more people die from the impacts of tropical cyclones in LEDCs compared to MEDCs.

....

....

....

....

....

....

....

....

Exercise 6.6 Review of natural hazards

In this exercise you will have an opportunity to review what you know about natural hazards by completing a crossword puzzle.

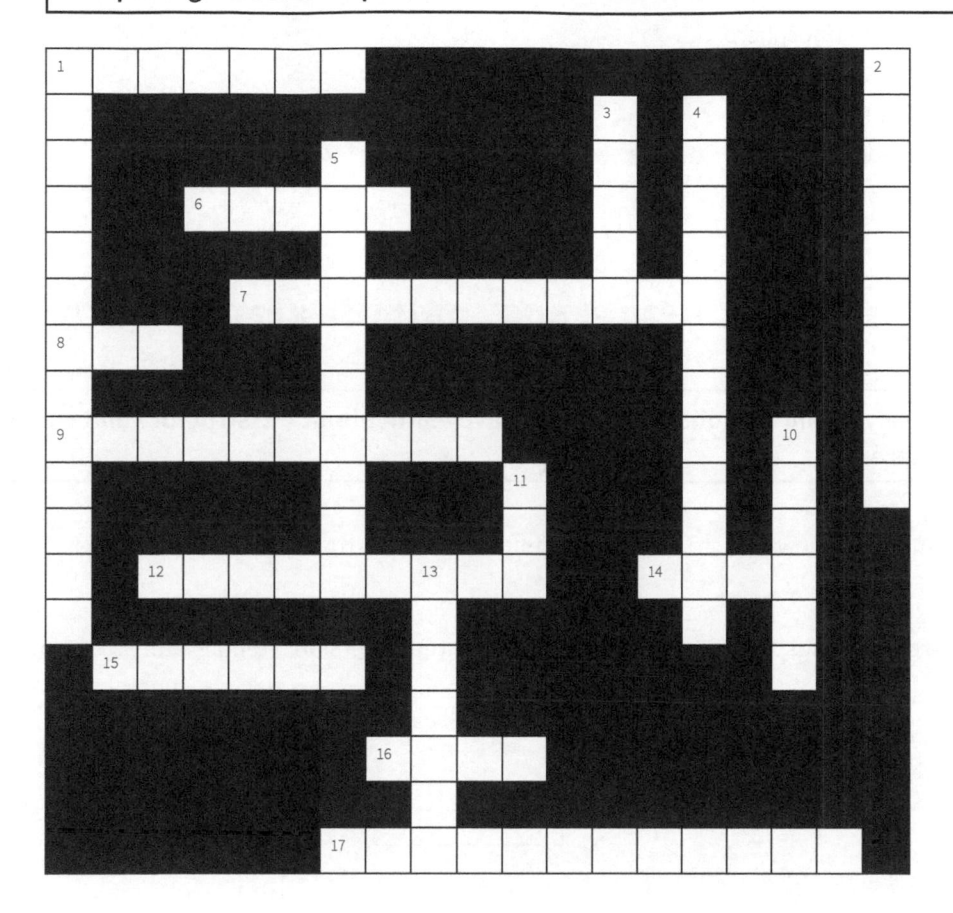

ACROSS

1 A tidal wave generated by seismic waves. (7)

6 A volcanic mudflow. (5)

7 Tectonic plates are made of this. (11)

8 Help given after an event in the form of food, medicine, etc. (3)

9 A rapid rise in sea level caused by a tropical cyclone. (5, 5)

12 The point on the Earth's surface above the focus of an earthquake. (9)

14 The name of the layer which forms the centre of the Earth. (4)

15 Oceanic crust is made up of mainly this rock. (6)

16 The name for the type of mountains found at a destructive plate boundary. (4)

17 The name of the plate boundary when two plates move away from each other. (12)

DOWN

1 A weather event that forms over tropical oceans of 27 degrees centigrade. (8, 5)

2 The name of the zone where one plate is deflected down into the mantle. (10)

3 Another name for a embankment that prevents flooding. (5)

4 A word to describe what happens when soil loses its stability during an earthquake. (12)

5 A violent shaking of the Earth's crust. (10)

10 The type of volcano found at constructive plate boundaries. (6)

11 The name of the area of calm weather in a tropical cyclone. (3)

13 The name for tropical cyclones in the western Pacific. (7)

This chapter covers the following topics:

- structure and composition of the atmosphere
- causes of atmospheric pollution
- impacts of atmospheric pollution
- management of atmospheric pollution.

Exercise 7.1 The structure and composition of the atmosphere

> In this exercise you will consolidate what you have learnt about the structure and composition of the atmosphere.

1   The diagram below shows the structure of the atmosphere. Fill in the blank boxes on the diagram using the list below.

mesosphere   thermosphere   stratopause   temperature inversion   temperature   tropopause
pressure   stratosphere   mesopause   troposphere

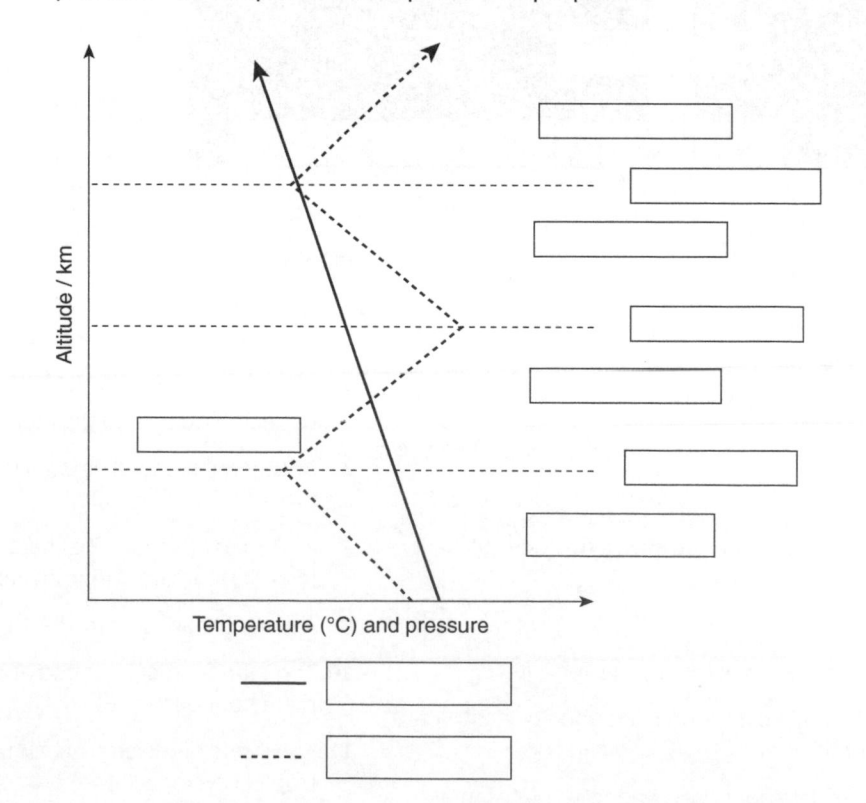

2   Complete the table using the appropriate letter from the list. There are ten possibilities and each letter should be used only once.

A   Oxygen

B   Carbon dioxide

C   Helium

D   Ozone

E   Nitrogen

F   Sulfur dioxide

G   Water vapour

H   Argon

I   Methane

J   Krypton

Statement	Letter
This gas is used by plants in photosynthesis.	
Ultraviolet radiation is absorbed by this gas.	
The most abundant gas in the atmosphere and a product of volcanic eruptions.	
This gas is produced by photosynthesis and is used in respiration.	
Keeping cattle can increase the level of this gas.	

3   The table below shows some pollutants in the atmosphere and their impacts. Tick the correct impact for the pollutant listed. The first one has been done for you.

Pollutants	Smog	Photochemical smog	Acid rain	Ozone depletion	Global climate change
Chlorine from CFCs				✓	
Sulfur dioxide and nitrogen oxide					
Carbon dioxide, tropospheric ozone, CFCs, methane					
Nitrogen oxide, tropospheric ozone, VOCs					
PM 10					

Exercise 7.2 Global climate change

This exercise will help you to improve your knowledge of the natural and enhanced greenhouse effect and global climate change. It will give you practice in calculating percentages and drawing line graphs and pie charts.

1 Use some of the words from the list below to complete the sentences about the natural greenhouse effect. Each word may be used once, more than once or not at all.

nitrogen   short-wave   absorbed   long-wave   carbon dioxide   emitted

Radiation from the Sun is called .... radiation. Almost half of

this radiation is .... by the Earth's surface and makes the Earth

warmer. .... radiation is ....

by the Earth. This radiation is .... by greenhouses gases such as

.... and the atmosphere heats up.

2 The two graphs below show changes in the concentration of carbon dioxide in the atmosphere and the global average surface temperatures.

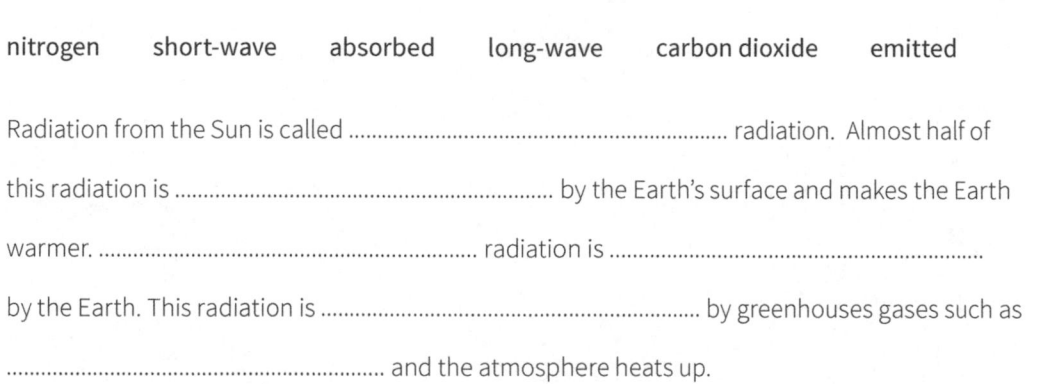

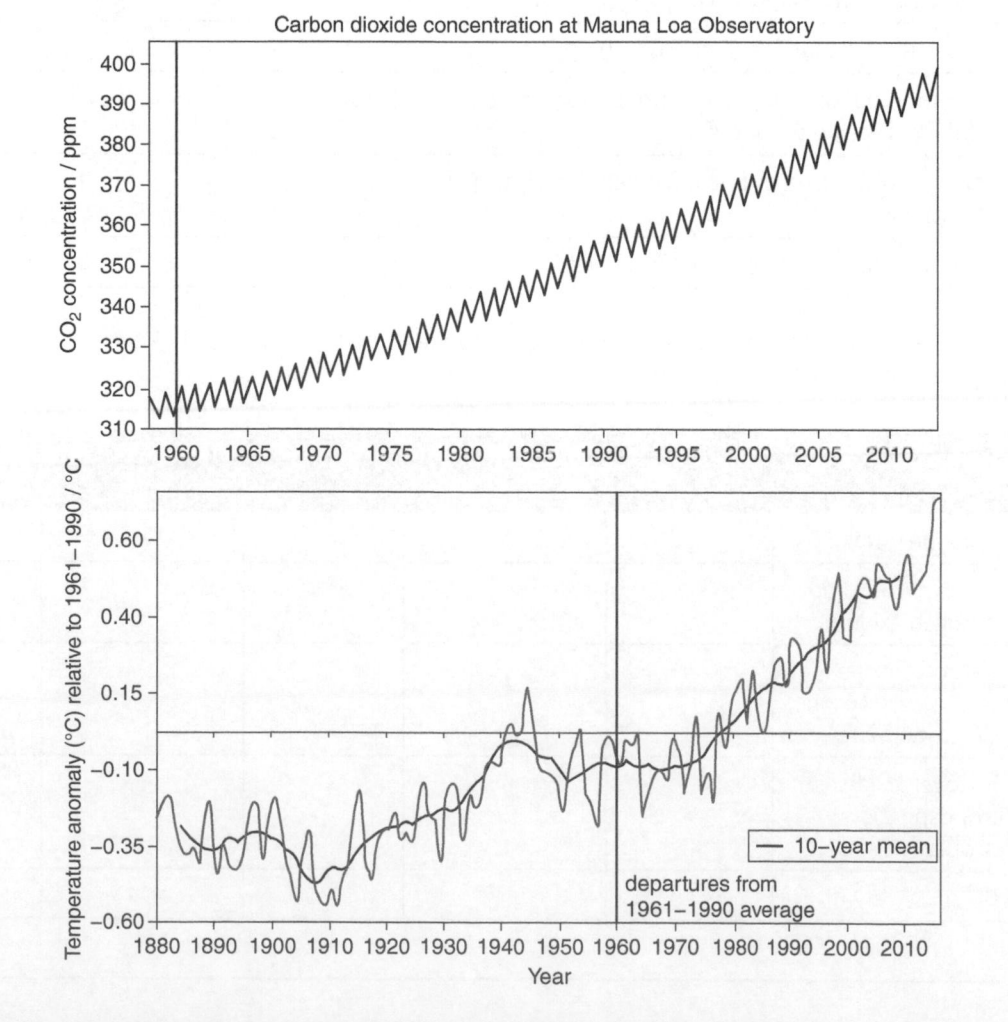

Describe the relationship between the concentration of carbon dioxide and the global average surface temperatures using evidence from the graphs.

....

....

....

....

3 Look again at the graph showing carbon dioxide concentration. Think about how carbon dioxide is produced and suggest why carbon dioxide concentration fluctuates during the year.

....

....

4 Explain why an increase in carbon dioxide concentration can lead to a change in the temperature of the atmosphere.

....

....

5 The list below shows the global carbon dioxide emissions by sector in 2013.

Residential	6%
Transport	23%
Industry	19%
Services	3%
Electricity generation	42%
Others	7%

Using the information complete the pie chart and key below.

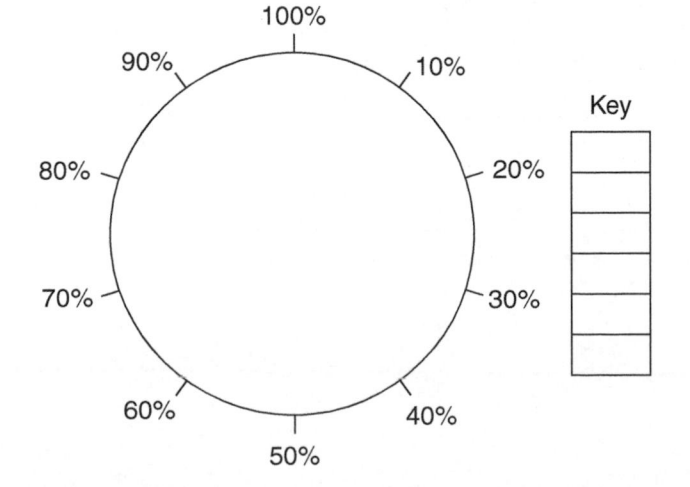

6 Which **two** sectors combined generated nearly two-thirds of global carbon dioxide emissions in 2013? Circle the correct answer from the options below.

transport and industry   electricity generation and industry

transport and electricity generation   transport and residential

7 As well as carbon dioxide, which other greenhouse gases are produced by the generation of electricity?

....

8 The table below shows carbon dioxide emissions (from the burning of fossils fuels and cement production) per capita, for selected countries between 1994 and 2014. The world average was 4.9 tonnes of CO_2 per person in 2014.

	Carbon emissions per capita (tonnes of CO_2)					
	1994	1998	2002	2006	2010	2014
World	4	4.1	4.1	4.7	4.8	4.9
China	2.6	2.7	2.9	4.9	6.2	7.1
United States of America	19.4	19.6	19.6	19.1	17.5	17
United Kingdom	9.4	9.1	8.9	8.9	7.8	6.7
India	0.9	1.1	1.1	1.3	1.6	2.0
Kenya	0.2	0.3	0.2	0.3	0.3	0.3
Bangladesh	0.2	0.2	0.2	0.3	0.4	0.4

Plot a line graph to show the data in the table on the grid below. The world average has already been plotted. Plot the points accurately and complete a key.

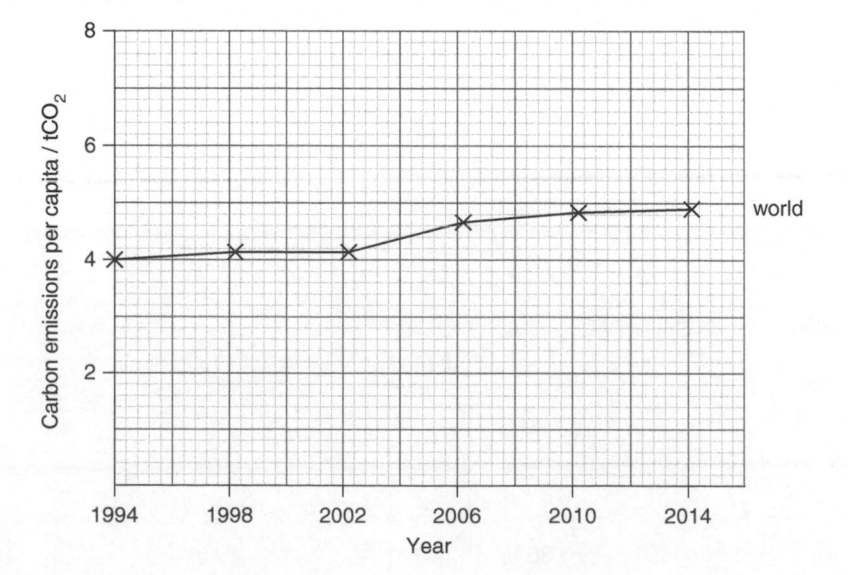

9 Using evidence from the line graph, describe the difference in the carbon dioxide emissions per capita between MEDCs and LEDCs between 1994 and 2014.

....

....

....

....

....

....

10 How many times greater were the carbon dioxide emissions per capita from the United States of America than from India in 2014? Circle the correct answer.

8 times   4 times   9 times   8.5 times   6 times

11 How many countries on the line graph were above the world average in 2014?

....

....

....

12 Suggest reasons for the difference you noted in question 9.

....

....

....

....

....

....

13 The diagram below shows the possible impacts of global warming as a result of an increase in carbon dioxide emissions.

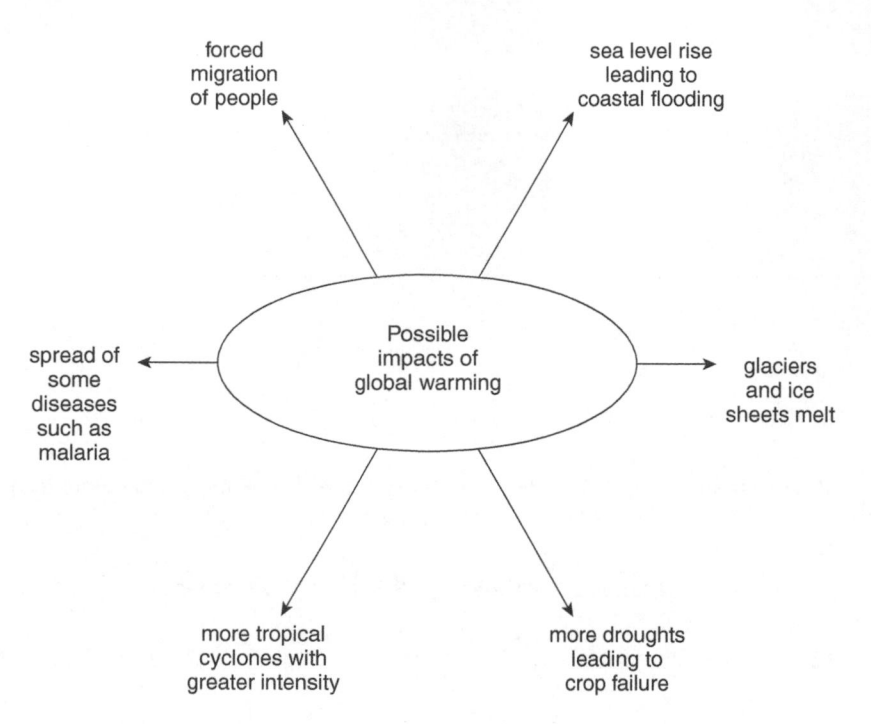

Suggest reasons why governments in some countries such as Bangladesh, which is not a major carbon dioxide emitter, are more concerned about global warming than other countries.

....

....

....

....

....

....

14 Describe international strategies for reducing carbon dioxide emissions.

....

....

....

....

Exercise 7.3 Ozone depletion

> This exercise will help you understand the causes, impacts and management strategies of ozone depletion.

1 What do you understand by the term 'the ozone hole'?

....

....

2 The graph below shows the maximum daily extent of the ozone depletion area between 1979 and 2014.

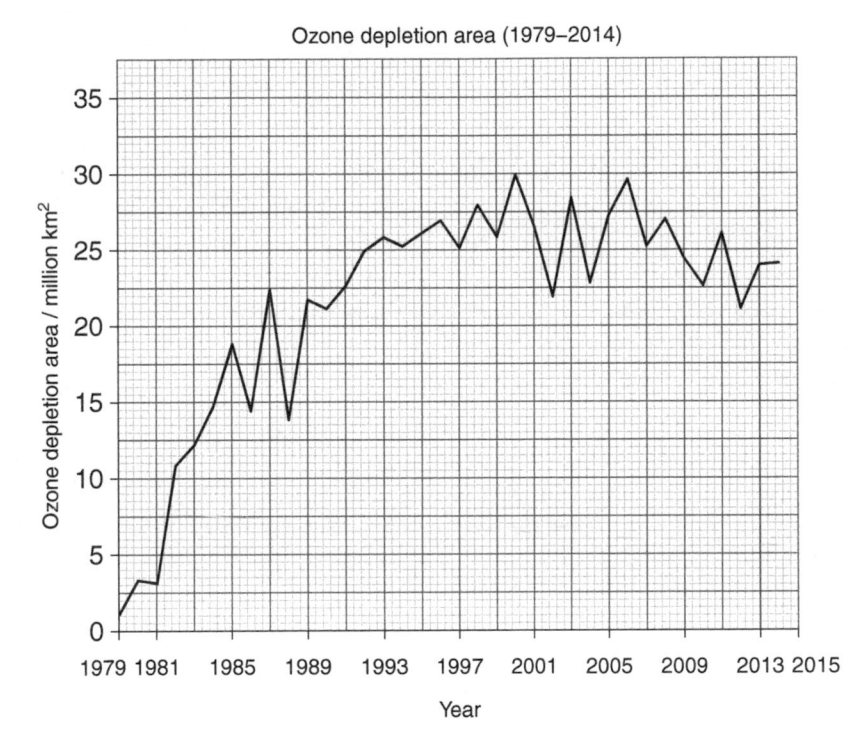

Ozone depletion area (1979–2014)

Describe the trend shown by the graph.

....

....

3 Name the main group of gases that caused ozone depletion.

....

4 Suggest how human activities increased the levels of these gases in the atmosphere.

....

....

5 Describe how the release of these gases caused ozone depletion.

....

....

6 Describe the possible impacts of reduced stratospheric ozone for life on Earth.

....

....

....

....

7 Describe the strategies used to prevent ozone depletion.

....

....

8 Explain why it will be many years before ozone depletion is no longer a problem.

....

....

Exercise 7.4 The causes, impacts and management of smog

This exercise will help you to improve your knowledge of the causes, impacts and management of an atmospheric pollution event: the South East Asian haze of 2015.

Read the newspaper extract below.

Haze chokes Singapore and neighbours

From June to the end of October, hazardous smog blanketed parts of northern Indonesia, Singapore and Malaysia. The smog was so dense that a woman in Singapore commented 'I can't even see what's happening outside my house'. South East Asia has suffered for years from annual events of smog caused by forest fires from illegal slash and burn farming on Sumatra and Kalimantan islands. The practice is used to clear land for rubber and palm oil plantations and paper and pulp. The peat soil is highly flammable and fires soon get out of control. The fires were made worse in 2015 by the effects of the El Nino weather phenomenon, leading to a prolonged dry season which dried out the soil, fuelling the flames further.

In Indonesia, 180,000 people reported irritation of the eyes, throat, lungs and skin. Schools closed, flights were cancelled and the number of deaths from traffic accidents increased due to poor visibility. Tourism declined and the government estimated $47 billion was lost to the economy because of a decline in agricultural production and trade. The environment also suffered: orangutans lost their homes and large amounts of carbon dioxide emissions were released.

In Singapore, schools were also closed and flights delayed. Elderly and vulnerable people were warned to avoid strenuous activity and free face masks were provided. The swimming World Cup was cancelled and the Singapore Grand Prix was also threatened with cancellation.

The immediate response to the forest fires was the deployment of 21,000 troops to tackle the flames. Cloud seeding was attempted and helicopters water bombed the worst fires. Retention basins for water were also constructed. Suggested longer term responses were to provide farmers with assistance to pursue alternative practices of forest management. An online land registry was set up to ease the identification of those responsible for starting the fires and big companies were encouraged to sign zero deforestation pledges. The Singapore government fined companies up to $1.6 million if they were found guilty of causing the smog. The government also established a smog early warning system via mobile apps and the internet and has an education programme so people know how to protect themselves during a smog event.

Look at the map which shows the extent of the South East Asian smog in September 2015.

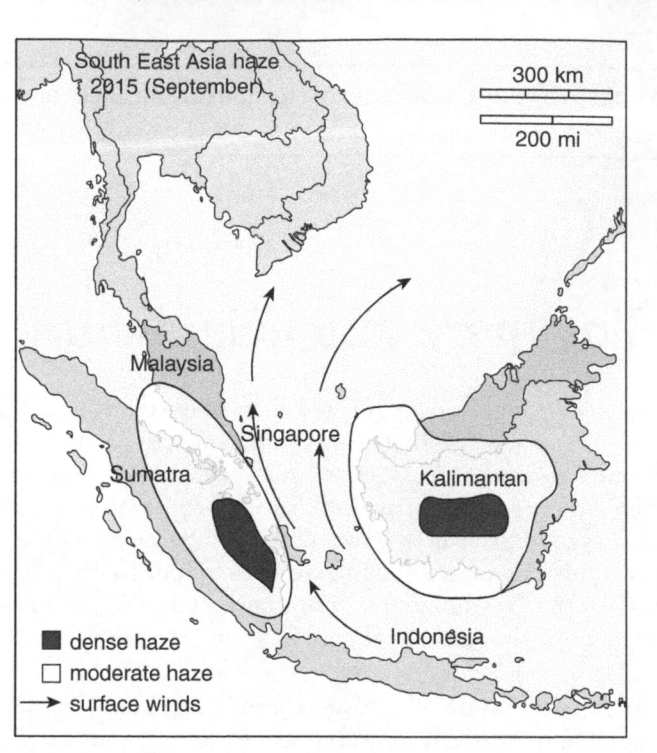

1 Describe where the South East Asian smog in September 2015 was located.

....

....

2 Estimate the area that the smog covered and circle the correct answer below.

   1 million km²   5 million km²   1.3 million km²   4.5 million km²

3 In which direction was the smog travelling and why?

....

....

4 What was the main cause of the smog?

....

....

5 Air quality in Singapore is measured by the Pollution Standards Index (PSI). PSI measures PM2.5, PM10, sulfur dioxide, nitrogen dioxide, ozone and carbon monoxide levels. The table below shows how the PSI values are related to air quality and daily activity.

24-hour PSI value	Air quality	Health Advisory
<100	Good to moderate	Normal activities
101 to 200	Unhealthy	The elderly, pregnant women and children should minimise prolonged outdoor activities.
201 to 300	Very unhealthy	People with lung and heart disease should avoid outdoor activity.
300+	Hazardous	All people should avoid outdoor activity.

Using the data from the table below, plot on the grid the maximum average PSI values at 12 p.m. on days when Singapore was worst affected by the smog. The minimum values have already been plotted for you.

September 2015									October 2015								
22	23	24	25	26	27	28	29	30	1	2	3	4	5	6	7	8	9
85	119	216	306	110	76	150	214	169	201	145	161	133	129	182	130	80	89

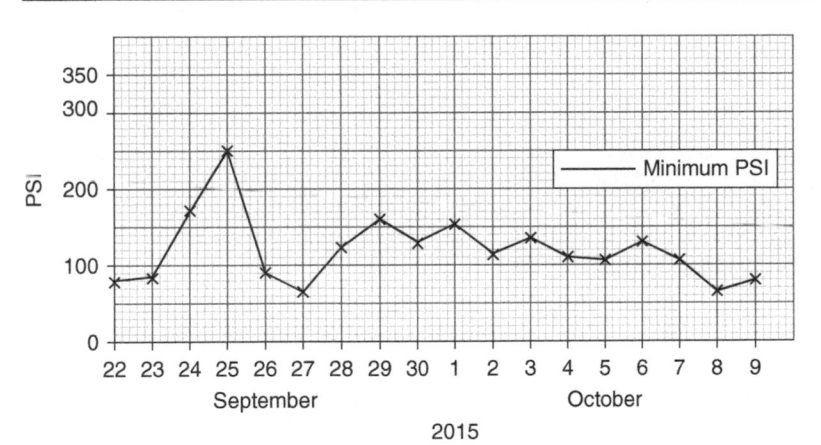

6 Draw a line on your graph to show when the PSI value indicates hazardous air quality and a second line to show when the PSI value indicates very unhealthy air quality.

7 For how many days during the time period plotted should all people have avoided outdoor activity?

....

8 For how many days was the air quality over Singapore regarded as very unhealthy?

....

9 Use evidence from the graph to suggest on what day the smog started to lessen over Singapore. Explain your answer.

....

....

10 Is there an anomalous result in the maximum average PSI values you have plotted and, if so, can you suggest reasons why?

....

....

11 Describe **four** impacts of the smog.

....

....

....

....

12 Why is it difficult to reduce air pollution in urban areas such as Singapore?

....

....

....

....

13 Describe the strategies used to manage the smog in South East Asia.

....

....

....

....

....

14 A student planned a study about the amount of carbon particles in the air in a town. The following method was used.

   A   Expose for 24 hours.

   B   Fix hardboard above ground level.

   C   Place squares of sticky tape on hardboard.

   D   Cut out squares of sticky tape.

   E   Ensure side of hardboard with the sticky tape is exposed to the air.

   F   Collect hardboard and use a hand magnifying lens to count the number of black carbon particles on each square of sticky tape.

The student did not write the method in the correct order. Complete the table below to show the correct order.

					F

15 Suggest a suitable sampling method the student could have used to select the sites in the town to collect the data.

....

....

16 Suggest why the student exposed the hardboard for 24 hours.

....

....

17 Suggest one piece of information that should have been included in the method so that the study could be repeated fairly.

....

....

18 The student proposed three different plans that could be used to carry out the survey.

Plan A   Pick 5 sites in the town. Expose hardboard for 24 hours.

Plan B   Pick 10 sites in the town. Expose hardboard for 24 hours once a week for two weeks.

Plan C   Pick 10 sites in five different areas of the town. Expose hardboard for 24 hours once a week for four weeks.

Suggest why Plan A may give the least reliable data.

....

....

....

19 Give reasons why Plan C is better than Plans A and B.

....

....

....

....

20 Suggest one other piece of data the student could also collect at the sampling sites to help with the analysis of the amount of carbon particles in the air.

....

....

Exercise 7.5 The causes, impacts and management of acid rain

This exercise will check your knowledge of acid rain, as well as giving you more practice in drawing bar graphs and analysing data.

1   Sulfur dioxide and nitrogen oxide are two gases that cause acid rain (pH 5.6). Name one natural source of a gas that can lead to acid rain.

....

2 Look at the divided bar graph which shows sources of sulfur dioxide emissions in the United States of America in 2015.

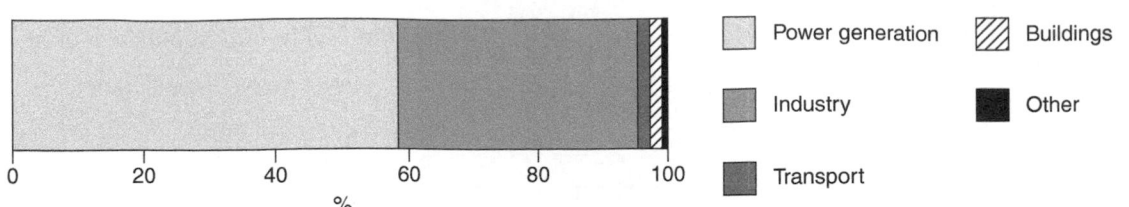

Which source produced the highest sulfur dioxide emissions in 2015?

....

3 The table below shows the % of nitrogen oxide emitted by sources in the United States in 2015. Complete the table.

Source of nitrogen oxide	Percentage
transport	45
industry	
power generation	10
buildings	7
other	6

4 Complete a divided bar graph below on the grid to show the sources of nitrogen oxide emissions in the United States of America in 2015.

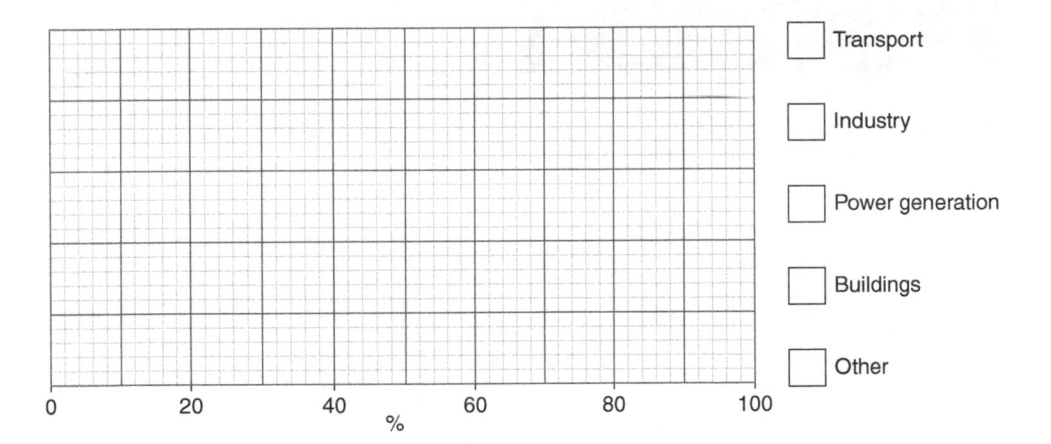

5 Using the statements below, complete the flow chart to show the cause of acid rain. The statements are not in the correct order.

falls to Earth as acid rain

sulfur dioxide and nitrogen oxides released

dry deposition

gases mix with water vapour and oxygen in the atmosphere

blown by wind over large distances

weak solutions of nitric and sulfuric acids

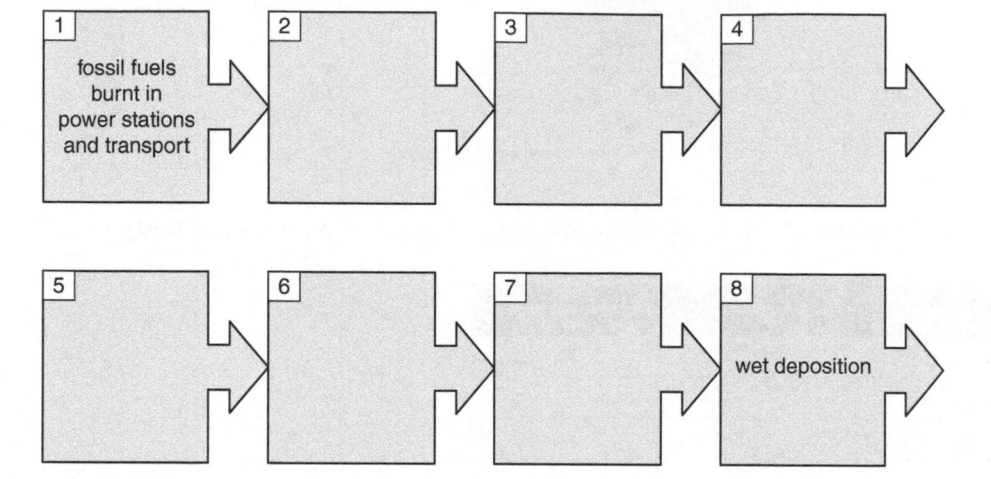

| 1 fossil fuels burnt in power stations and transport | 2 | 3 | 4 |

| 5 | 6 | 7 | 8 wet deposition |

6 The Adirondack Park is in the north east of the United States of America. It covers 24 281 square kilometres. 27% of the 2800 lakes within the Park have a pH of less than 5. A researcher decided to investigate how pH levels in some of the lakes of the Park affect the number of fish species. The results are shown below.

Number of fish species in lakes tested	7	118	154	297	96
pH value in lakes tested	4	5	6	7	8

How many times greater was the number of fish species when the pH of the lake was 7 compared to the lakes with a pH value of 5? Circle the correct answer.

2   1.5   2.5   3   4

7 Does the data suggest that pH had an effect on fish species? Use information from the table to support your answer.

....

....

....

....

8 Suggest one other measurement the researcher could have recorded to investigate the impact of pH values on fish populations in a lake.

....

....

....

....

9 Describe the impact of acid rain on crops and vegetation.

....

....

....

....

....

....

10 Look at the diagrams which show sulfur and nitrogen concentrations in the United States of America in 1985 and 2014.

1985
- 0–30
- 30–60
- 60–90
- 90 +

2014
(μeq/L)
- 0–30
- 30–60
- 60–90
- 90 +

sulfur + nitrogen concentration

Describe the pattern shown for sulfur and nitrogen concentrations between 1985 and 2014.

....

....

....

11 It has been estimated that by 2040 sulfur dioxide and nitrogen oxide emissions in the United States of America will have fallen by 50% of 2015 emission levels. Describe and explain **three** strategies that could lead to this reduction of emissions.

....

....

....

....

....

....

12 It has been estimated that by 2040 sulfur dioxide and nitrogen oxide emissions in India will have increased by 10% of 2015 emission levels. Why are strategies for reducing acid rain more likely to be effective in MEDCs than in LEDCs?

....

....

....

....

....

....

Exercise 7.6 A review of atmospheric pollution

In this exercise you will review what you know about atmospheric pollution by completing a crossword puzzle.

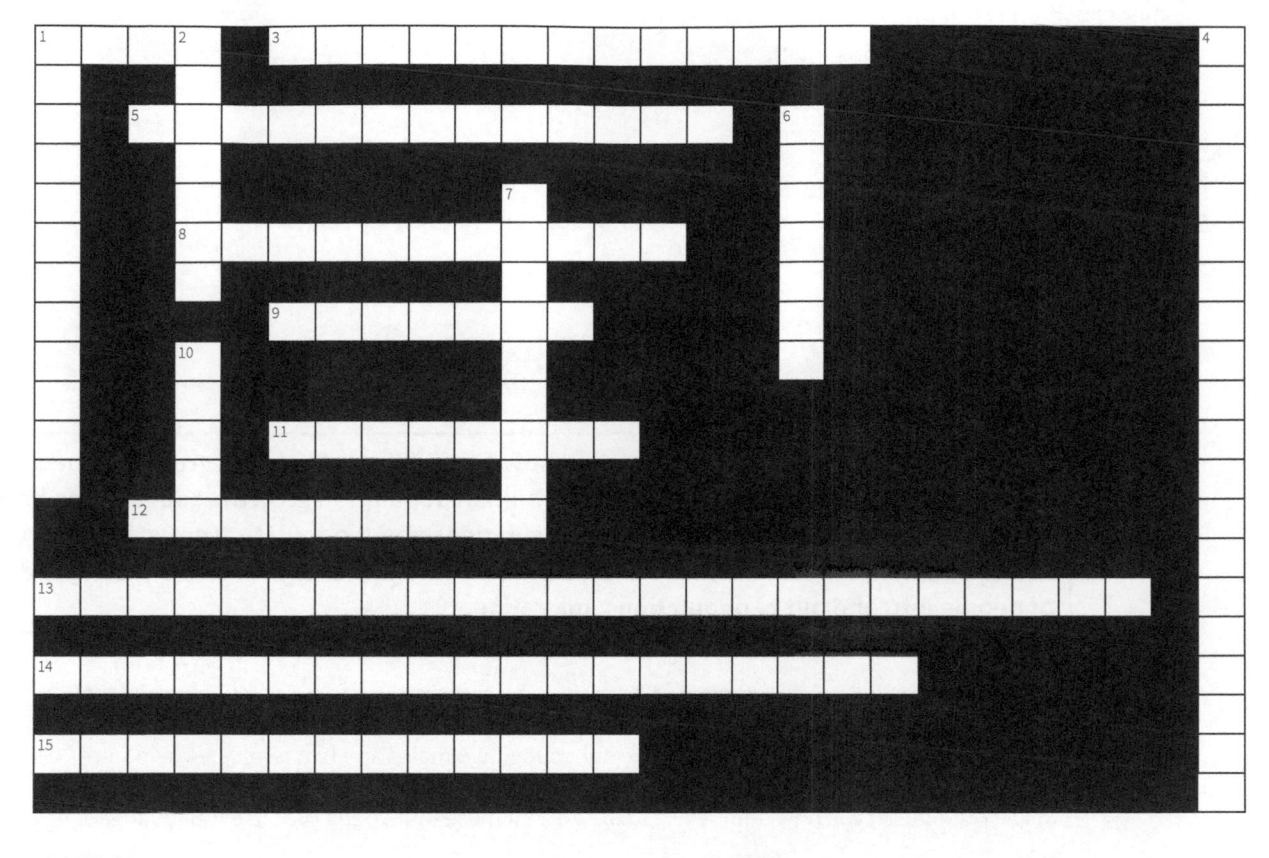

ACROSS

1 A mixture of smoke and fog. (4)

3 The type of smog that increases in sunny conditions. (13)

5 A gas used by plants in photosynthesis. (6, 7)

8 Lowest layer of the atmosphere. (11)

9 The name given to pollutants that directly pollute the atmosphere. (7)

11 The name of precipitation with a pH value of less than 6. (4, 4)

12 The upper limit of the mesosphere. (9)

13 Chemicals that enter the atmosphere as gases from evaporation. (8, 7, 9)

14 The Montreal Protocol banned the use of these gases. (19)

15 A gas that contributes to acid rain. (6, 7)

DOWN

1 Ozone is concentrated in this atmospheric layer. (12)

2 The force which holds the atmosphere to Earth. (7)

4 When temperature increases with height. (11, 9)

6 Individuals can be encouraged to reduce, reuse and .... (7)

7 The radiation that is emitted from the Sun. (9)

10 Ultraviolet radiation is absorbed by this gas. (5)

Human population

Exercise 8.1   Changes in population size

This exercise will help you to understand how populations of animals grow and the similarities and differences between this pattern and human population growth. You will also have the chance to practise some mathematical calculations about population growth and birth and death rates. Finally, the exercise will help in your understanding of the factors affecting the movement of people into and out of populations: migration.

1   Complete the following passage by filling in the numbers in the gaps. A pair of animals, male and female, is

introduced into an area. They produce four young, two males and two females. The parents die after 1 year.

The population will now number .... If these four young produce four young for each pair, and

then die, the population will be .... after 2 years. If the pattern repeats itself, the population will be

.... after 5 years, 512 after .... years and .... after 10 years.

2   Plot the population numbers for years 1-10 on the graph below.

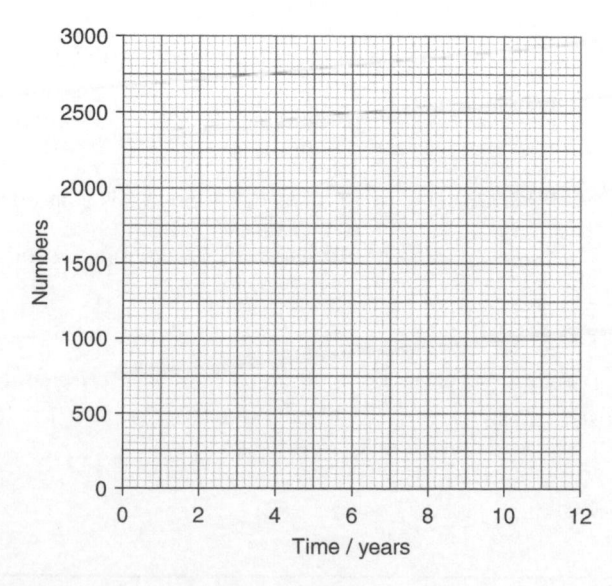

3 What name do we give to this type of population growth?

....

4 In a different colour on your graph, show what would happen when the population reached the carrying capacity of the environment if the carrying capacity of the environment were 3000.

5 The diagram shows estimated past population, actual population records up to 2010 and three possible predictions until 2100.

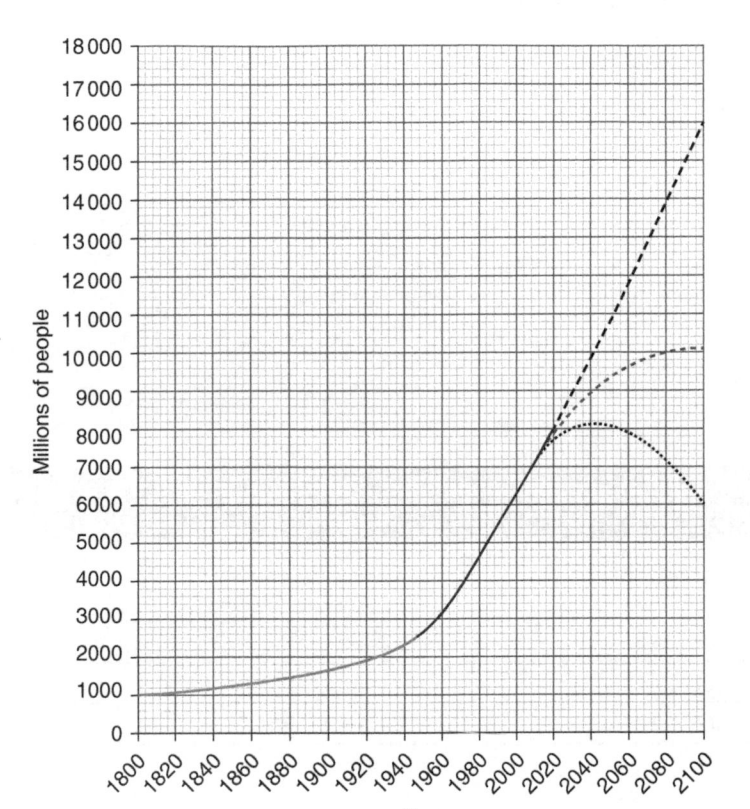

--- U.N. high ··· U.N. medium ····· U.N. low — actual — estimated

Answer the following questions.

a For how many years had the size of the human population been recorded up to 2010?

....

b What was the estimated population in 1800?

....

c i At what date was the human population 2 billion, and at what date was it at 4 billion?

   ii Approximately how long did the population take to double in size from 2 billion?

....

....

....

d What will be the doubling time, if any, from 2010 in the case of each of the predictions?

Low: ....

Medium: ....

High: ....

e Give **two** reasons for the change between 1800 and 2000.

....

....

....

....

....

6 Complete the table.

Population	Birth rate per year	Death rate per year	Increase / decrease per year	Increase / decrease percentage
1 000 000	10 000	5000	Increase by 5000 per year	Increase by 0.5%
10 000 000	50 000	30 000		
5 000 000	80 000		Increase by 20 000 per year	
20 000 000	150 000		Increase by 50 000 per year	Increase by 0.25 %
15 000 000	100 000			Decrease by 0.1 %

7 a Populations change in size due to migration, which includes immigration and emigration. The list shows push and pull factors. Decide which are push and which are pull. Put the factors in the correct column in the table.

A Not enough jobs

B Attractive climate

C Poor medical care

D Desertification

E Better educational opportunities

F More services and amenities

G Drought

H Better job opportunities

I Political freedom

J High levels of pollution

K Poor housing

L War

Push	Pull

b Which of type of factor, push or pull, would be most important in a less economically developed country (LEDC)? Explain your answer.

....

....

8 The following passage describes changes in a delta town affected by dam building on the river.

> In 1985 the river here was 4 km wide but is now only about 300 m. Up until about 1985 the summer floods deposited silt every year. Now, the sea is entering the delta land and many soils are useless for farming. Apart from farming, the region used to get its main income from fishing and shrimp collecting. The only fishermen remaining now catch a few crabs at sea. Most people spend the day collecting firewood.

This delta town has seen its population fall from 14 000 in 1980 to fewer than 2500 now. Explain whether push or pull factors are likely to account for this migration from the town.

....

....

....

....

9 **a** Assuming that b = birth rate, d = death rate, circle which of the following would apply when the population was growing.

b > d   b < d   b = d

b One of the rarest birds in North America is the whooping crane. By 1941, hunting and habitat loss meant that only 22 birds remained. Conservation measures were brought into place and the wild population has been growing ever since. The table shows counts of whooping cranes done every 10 years since 1940. An extra count for 2015 is also shown.

Year	Whooping crane population
1940	22
1950	34
1960	33
1970	56
1980	76
1990	146
2000	177
2010	281
2015	329

The graph shows the same data. Complete the graph using the information in the table.

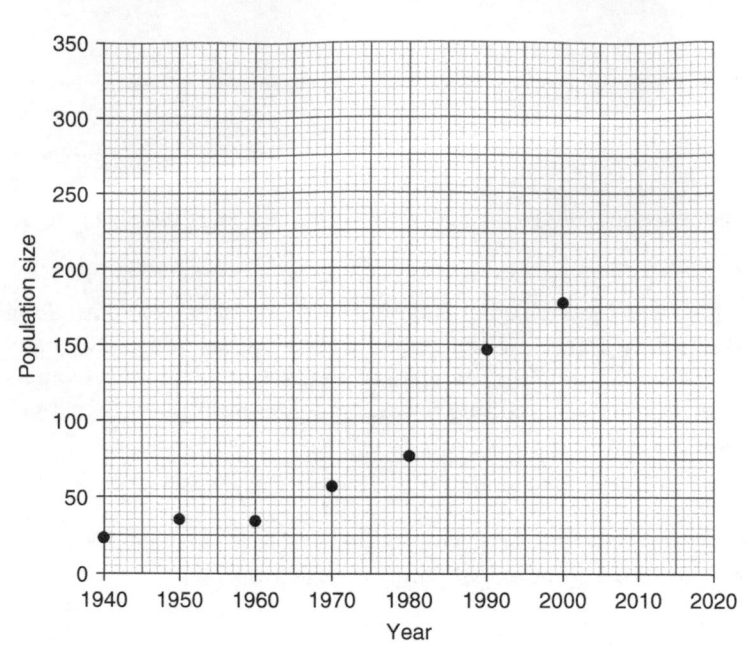

c The cranes migrate along a narrow route from their single breeding ground in Canada to their over-wintering site in Southern Texas.

Suggest how the data in the table could have been obtained.

....

....

d In which decade did the crane population increase the most?

....

e Calculate the overall rate of increase from 1940 until 2015. Show your working.

10 a Poisons, such as disinfectants, can affect many aspects of the biology of living things. One of these is population growth.

A student planned a study on the effect of a common household disinfectant on the growth of populations of an alga called *Chlorella*. This alga has microscopic cells.

The plan was written out in bullet points.

- Make up solutions of the disinfectant of different concentrations.

- Add a drop of a suspension of algae in water to each of the solutions.

- Take a small drop of the algal culture from each of the concentrations every day for a week.

- Estimate the number of cells in the drop using a microscope.

The student's teacher said that the plan needed improvement.

Suggest **three** problems with the plan and how it might be improved.

....

....

....

....

....

....

....

b The results of the study are shown in the graph. Describe the relationship shown in this graph.

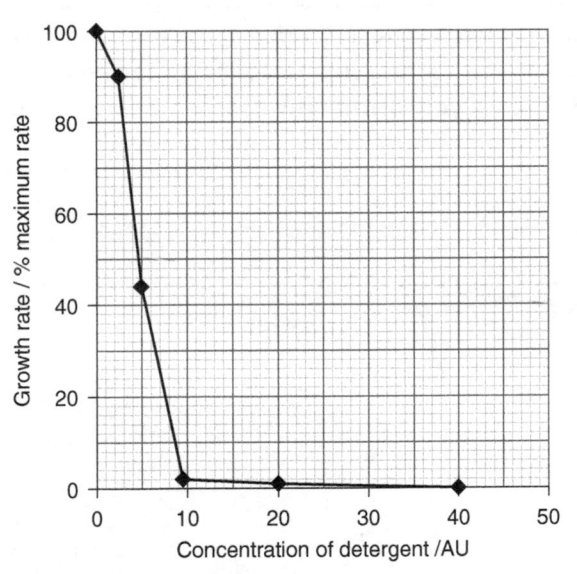

....

....

....

c   Suggest the value, in AU, that a government set as the maximum permitted in the lakes and rivers of this disinfectant. Assume that they aim to ensure that algal growth is not reduced by more than 10% anywhere. Show how you arrived at your answer by marking on the graph.

....

....

....

....

....

....

Exercise 8.2 Human population distribution and density

This exercise will give you practice at writing descriptions of the distribution of people around the world. If you know the names of the continents, your description can be written in terms of those. It will also give you a chance to practise your arithmetic abilities and to use the results of your calculations for a purpose.

1   Look at the diagram. Write a description of the distribution of the human population.

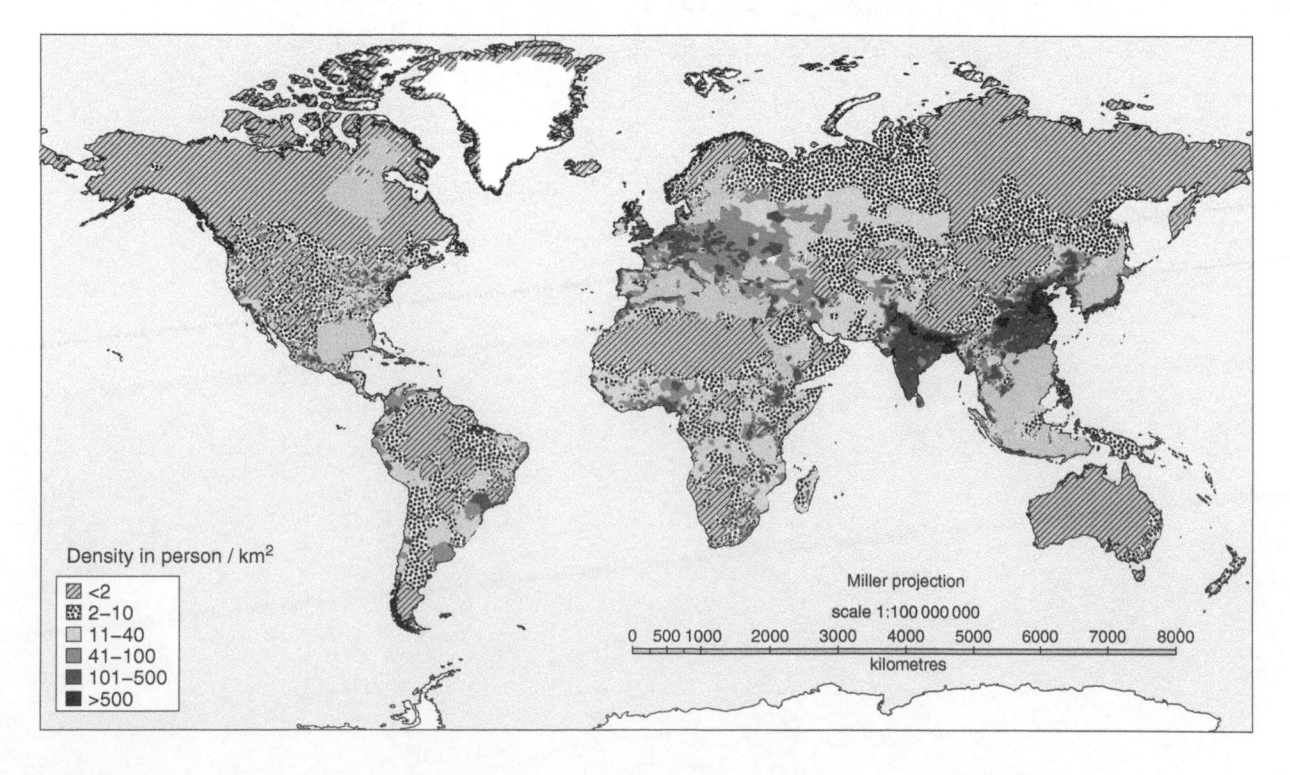

Density in person / km²

<2
2–10
11–40
41–100
101–500
>500

Miller projection

scale 1:100 000 000

0   500 1000   2000   3000   4000   5000   6000   7000   8000

kilometres

....

....

....

....

....

....

2 Brazil had a population of 203 657 210 in 2015. The area of Brazil is 8.52 million km². Calculate the density of the Brazilian population in 2015.

....

....

3 Bangladesh had a population of 160 411 249 in 2015. The area of Bangladesh is 147 570 km². Calculate how many times more dense the population of Bangladesh is compared to that of Brazil.

....

....

4 The table shows information about the population and areas of the seven provinces of Costa Rica. Calculate the density of these 7 provinces and add these data to the last column of the table. State which is the highest and which the lowest.

Province	Area (km²)	Population	Density (people per km²)
Heredia	2657	433 677	
Cartago	3124	490 903	
San José	4966	1 404 242	
Limón	9189	386 862	
Alajuela	9757	885 571	
Guanacaste	10 141	354 154	
Puntarenas	11 266	410 929	

....

....

....

....

....

....

....

Exercise 8.3 Population structure

This exercise will help you understand the basic types of population structure related to countries with different levels of economic development.

1 Sketch a population pyramid for a country in which the population is

   a declining

   b growing.

2 Compare the structure of the population pyramids for the two countries shown below.

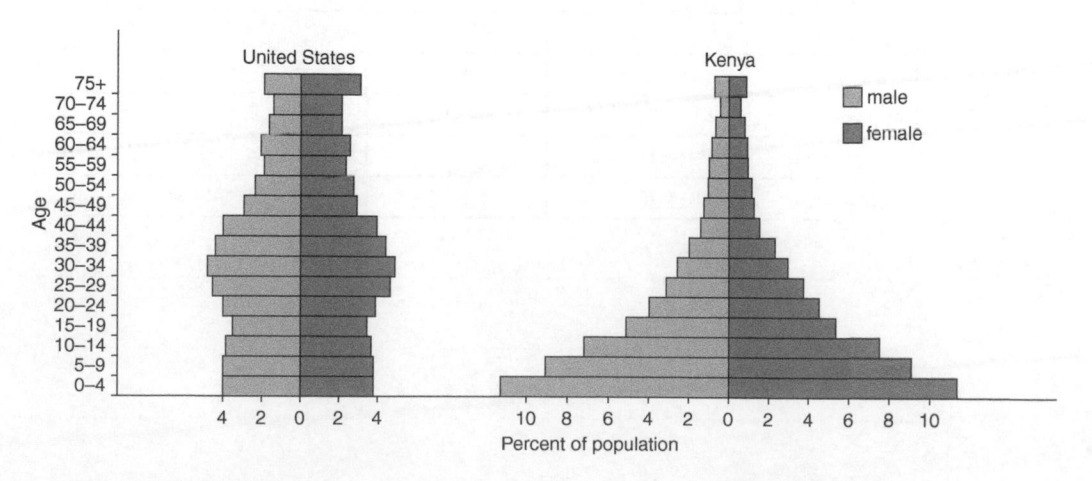

....

....

....

3 Explain what is meant by the term 'dependent' in relation to a population pyramid.

....

....

....

....

....

4 Explain the difference between a 'population pyramid' and a 'pyramid of numbers'.

....

....

5 Look at the population pyramid.

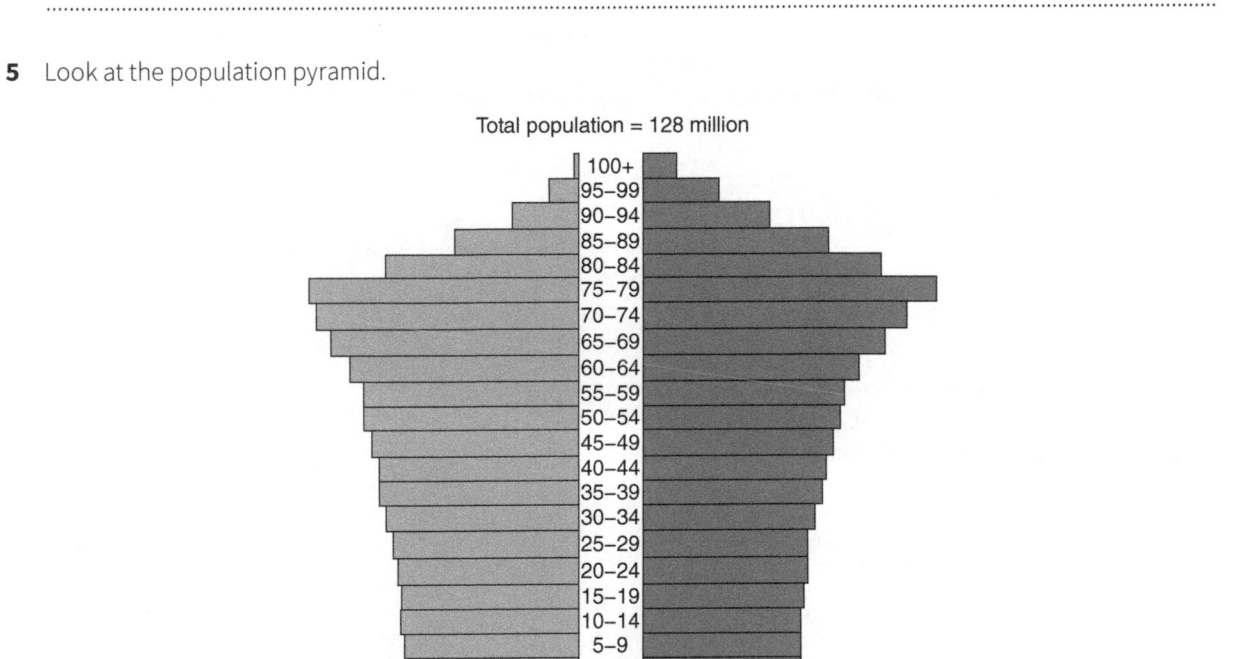

Total population = 128 million

Population / millions

male female

a Determine the population of males who are aged 14 and under.

b Calculate the percentage of the population who are female aged between 80 and 84.

....

Exercise 8.4 Managing human populations

Understanding population growth and structure allows populations to be managed for the benefit of people and the environment. This exercise will help you to check your understanding of the ways in which this can be achieved. This can be at the level of an individual couple, through to national governments.

1   Give **three** ways in which education may limit population growth.

....

....

....

....

....

....

2   Explain the difference between family planning and contraception.

....

....

....

....

3   Explain why measures which reduce death rate, such as improving sanitation, may also lead to a decrease in birth rate.

....

....

....

....

4   Suggest why a country may adopt a pro-natalist policy to manage its population.

....

....

....

5 Give **two** reasons, apart from contraception, why population growth rates are low in MEDCs.

....

....

....

....

....

....

Chapter 9:
Natural ecosystems and human activity

This chapter covers the following topics:

- ecosystem structure and function
- sampling and conserving biodiversity
- the causes of the loss of habitats and the loss of forests
- the effects of habitat and forest loss
- the sustainable management of forests.

Exercise 9.1 The ecosystem

This exercise will help you to understand the structure and function of ecosystems. The science of ecology, which studies ecosystems, has much of its own terminology. This exercise will also help you to learn the meanings of these new terms. It will consider the movement of food, and the energy and materials that it contains, through eaters and the eaten in an ecosystem. There are also some simple mathematical calculations, which will help you with this aspect.

1   Write down accurate definitions of these terms:

ecosystem

....

....

population

....

....

community

....

....

habitat

....

....

niche

....

....

2 Name **two** biotic and **two** abiotic factors for a woodland ecosystem.

....

....

....

....

....

3 Arrange these pH values in order from acid to alkaline.

5   11   2   8

....

4 A diagram which shows how food, energy and materials pass from one single species to another single

species is called a ....

5 A diagram which shows the number of living things at each feeding level in an

ecosystem is a ....

6 If we interlink a number of (answer to question 4) we get a ....

7 On a rocky beach barnacles feed on plankton. Dog whelks eat barnacles and mussels. The mussels also feed on plankton. Mussels are commonly eaten by starfish. Dog whelks and starfish are eaten by birds, such as oystercatchers.

Draw a food web for the rocky beach, using the information in the passage above.

8 In a survey of an area of rocky beach, the following figures were found:

barnacles   1 000 000

dog whelks   100

mussels   20

oystercatchers   1

starfish   3

Sketch a pyramid of numbers for this part of the ecosystem. On your sketch, show the actual numbers at each level.

9 The survey was unable to get figures for the primary producers for this pyramid. Explain why this might have been the case.

....

....

....

....

10 The equation for respiration is opposite to that for ....

11 Explain in detail why a plant given water, carbon dioxide and a light source (all the requirements for the manufacture of glucose by the plant) would still not grow very well.

....

....

....

....

....

12 State the name of the biotic interaction which is happening in each of the following pictures.

a   b   c

....

....

....

13 Briefly explain the role of chlorophyll in nature.

....

....

....

....

14 Complete the table using the information given in it, and the data from question 8 (page 136). Then use the information from your completed table to draw a pyramid of energy for this ecosystem.

Organism	Mass of one specimen	Energy content / kJ per gram	Total energy in the area / kJ
barnacle	50 mg	6	
mussel	10 g	7	
dog whelk	5 g	5	
starfish	0.5 kg	8	
oystercatcher	0.5 kg	10	

15 On this diagram of the carbon cycle, name substances A and C and processes B and D.

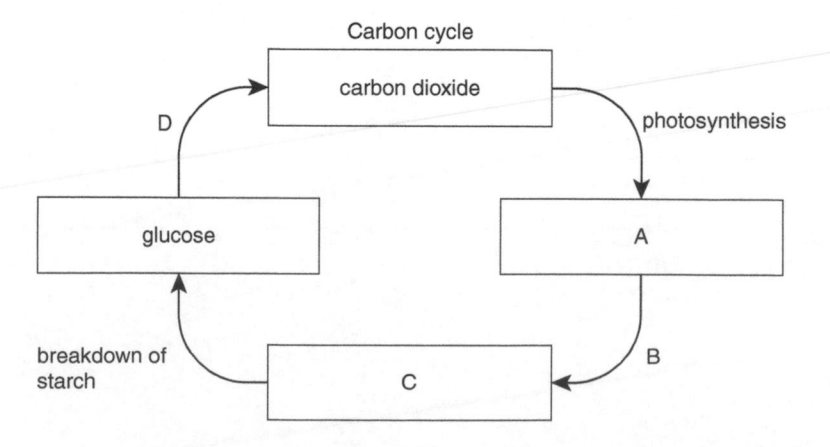

16 a Compare the processes of photosynthesis and respiration by discussing the substances which are used and those which are produced.

....

....

....

....

b Both photosynthesis and respiration involve energy. Compare the kind of energy involved in the two processes.

....

....

....

17 Two species of animals living in a fast-flowing stream are in competition with each other. Their basic requirements, as with most animals, are for food, oxygen and water. Suggest which one of these three requirements they are likely to be in competition for. Explain your answer.

....

....

....

....

....

Exercise 9.2 Estimating biodiversity in ecosystems

> This exercise will help you to understand some of the ways in which we can estimate the sizes of natural populations and get information about where they live. This is answering the *how* of what occurs where. After the *how* of what occurs is understood, it is possible to consider the *why*, e.g. why organisms live where they do and why they are rare or common. All this information is needed to formulate strategies for their conservation. The exercise will also help you to understand the different sampling methods and sampling types.

1   Ants have made a trail through some grassland. Explain how you could investigate the effect the ants have had on the vegetation on the trail compared to that on either side. Use a diagram to help your explanation.

    ....

    ....

    ....

    ....

    ....

2   Explain the meaning of the term 'biodiversity'.

    ....

    ....

    ....

3 Describe a situation in which you might use random number tables and a quadrat to sample some vegetation.

....

....

....

....

....

4 Match the sampling methods to the organisms in the following lists.

Organisms

a Barnacles stuck to rocks

b Lichens on tree trunks

c Ground beetles running around in a meadow

d Mosquitoes

Methods

A Pooter and net

B Quadrat

C Pitfall trap

....

....

....

....

5 The diagram below shows a grassland area surrounded by trees. Explain how you could sample the plants in the meadow. You also have access to a set of random number tables as shown.

	1	2	3	4	5	6	7	8	9	10	11	12
1	3	6	2	0	1	8	9	7	2	1	3	4
2	2	7	5	1	2	6	2	7	1	0	9	5
3	6	8	1	5	1	5	3	8	8	5	4	3
4	6	0	9	5	5	2	8	3	1	6	2	0
5	4	5	4	5	3	5	3	0	5	5	8	9
6	4	8	7	8	9	9	8	0	9	9	7	7
7	2	7	8	6	9	3	7	3	2	4	4	5
8	5	6	5	8	2	9	4	4	2	8	9	9
9	4	2	5	1	9	1	3	8	1	7	0	9
10	9	6	8	3	9	8	7	2	4	0	9	0
11	1	3	1	5	9	6	7	9	8	8	3	4
12	9	3	0	3	9	7	1	3	4	0	1	2
13	7	3	6	8	1	2	1	8	6	0	3	9
14	3	9	0	4	9	1	9	9	9	3	3	6
15	4	6	8	9	9	0	2	1	6	9	9	0
16	6	6	7	7	1	5	8	5	2	4	8	2
17	2	0	0	8	5	5	9	6	9	7	4	0
18	4	0	4	4	1	0	3	4	2	5	9	7
19	5	2	7	0	9	6	0	5	0	7	6	6
20	8	7	0	3	9	8	4	1	0	3	5	3
21	7	4	5	6	2	0	5	6	7	7	9	5
22	9	7	8	6	9	1	4	4	4	5	2	6
23	4	2	0	1	2	0	3	8	6	5	5	2
24	9	1	6	8	2	7	1	7	7	8	0	1
25	9	7	0	0	1	5	6	6	2	8	8	9
26	2	5	1	7	5	8	1	8	0	0	8	1
27	3	4	6	9	3	0	8	5	4	7	6	2
28	3	7	8	2	1	0	6	8	9	5	7	4
29	5	9	1	6	9	5	9	9	1	1	4	3
30	9	6	8	0	1	1	6	8	6	1	3	3

....

....

....

....

....

....

....

....

6 The diagram shows a section through a primary forest at the place where a firebreak has been cut.

Firebreaks are cut through forests to avoid the spread of fire from one block of forest to another. However, any removal of such valuable forest habitat is a concern. An ecologist carried out a survey using standard techniques to assess the impact of firebreak cutting on biodiversity in the forest shown.

The below diagram shows an aerial view of the firebreak and the surrounding forest.

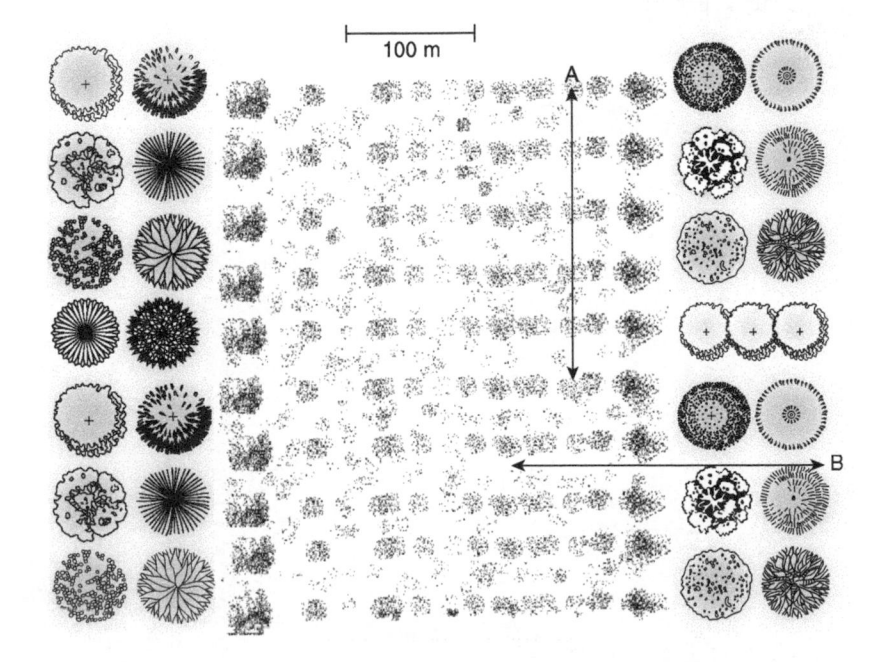

a The ecologist considered two possible transect positions to assess the effect, A and B. Explain why the ecologist chose position B.

....

....

....

....

b Calculate how many quadrats would be required to place one every 20 m along the transect line in Plan B.

....

....

....

....

c The diagram below shows a quadrat placed at 80 m from the start.

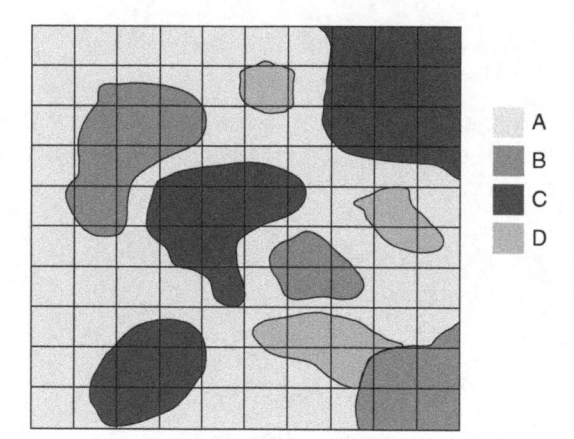

Estimate the cover of each plant species shown using the ACFOR scale. On this scale the following apply:

A = abundant

C = common

F = frequent

O = occasional

R = rare

This method is covered in more detail in Section 9.2 of the Coursebook.

....

....

....

....

d Use the quadrat in the diagram for part c to estimate percentage cover using any method you choose. Explain the method you have used and how you have applied it to this quadrat.

....

....

....

....

....

....

e Draw a table in which the results of the first five quadrats of Plan B could be recorded, assuming eight species were found (it would almost certainly be more than this).

f Both Plan B and Plan A use systematic sampling. Another ecologist suggested that the question about the effect of the firebreak on the biodiversity of the forest could be investigated using a random sampling technique. With reference to the diagram that shows an aerial view of the firebreak and the surrounding forest, suggest how a random sampling method could be used to help to answer this question.

....

....

....

....

....

....

Exercise 9.3 The causes and impacts of habitat loss

One of the biggest ecological problems the world faces is that of habitat loss. This can be due to such diverse causes as acquiring land for farming and housing, to climate change. This exercise will help you to understand the main causes of habitat loss and the problems that it can lead to.

1 If there are 50 million species on Earth, and the current extinction rate is 0.02% per year, then how many species will go extinct in a single year?

....

2 Describe **three** advantages of wetland habitats.

....

....

....

....

....

....

3 What are the major reasons for the drainage of wetlands?

....

....

....

....

....

4 Describe **one** reason for wetland loss that is not due to drainage.

....

....

....

5 The Pantanal in Brazil (140 000 km²), the Llanos of Venezuela and Colombia (about 500 000 km²) and the Pearl and Yangtze river deltas in China (650 000 km²) represent some of the world's major wetland areas. It is estimated that there are about 8 000 000 km² of wetland in the world. Calculate what percentage the three areas mentioned constitute of total world wetland area.

....

6   The table shows the causes of deforestation in the Brazilian rainforest.

Cause	Percentage
small-scale subsistence agriculture	33
cattle ranching	60
crop farming	1
logging	3
roads, dams, towns, mining	3

Display the data on a pie chart and include a key.

7   Use the data from question 6 and calculate the percentage loss due to agricultural practices.

8   Rich rainforest habitats such as the Amazon have great biodiversity. Habitat destruction causes a loss of biodiversity and therefore loss of genetic variation (genetic depletion).

Explain why genetic depletion is a problem.

....

....

....

....

....

Exercise 9.4 The causes and impacts of deforestation

The single biggest loss of habitat is that due to deforestation. Forests are the site of enormous biomass as well as biodiversity, and their loss has consequences beyond habitat loss. This exercise will help you think about all of the major problems caused by deforestation. It will also give you a chance to practise some maths.

1   Give **three** uses of wood.

   ....

   ....

   ....

   ....

   ....

2   The rate of deforestation in the Amazon basin is estimated to be 0.52% of the entire area per year. This is equivalent to 18 857 km². Calculate the total area of the Amazon basin.

   ....

3 A major factor driving deforestation is the construction of roads. A study looked at the relationship between distance from a road and the extent of deforestation, and also the effect of protection. The data are shown in the graph.

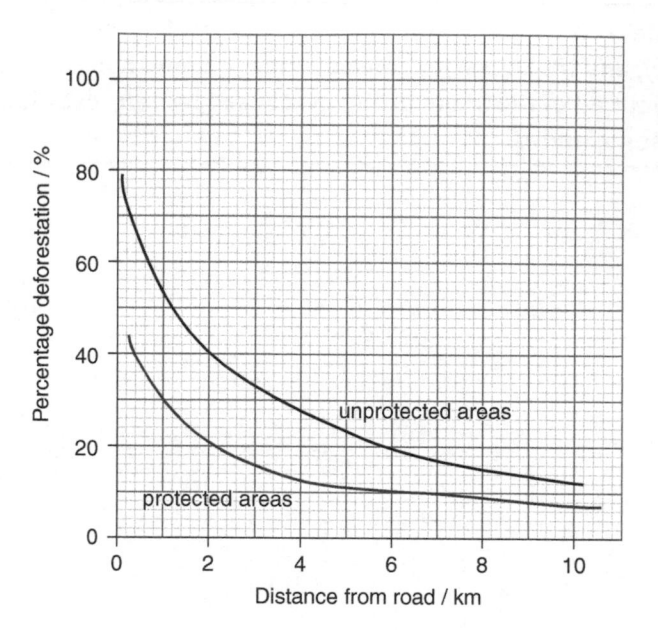

What is the percentage deforestation at 4 km from the road in a protected area and in an unprotected area?

....

....

....

....

....

4 Using the data in question 3, write a short account of the effect of road building and habitat protection on deforestation in the Amazon.

....

....

....

....

....

....

5   How do rainforests protect an area against soil erosion?

....

....

....

....

....

6   Carbon dioxide levels in the atmosphere are rising. The main cause of this rise is the burning of fossil fuels (87%). After this comes land use changes at 9%, and industry accounts for the remaining 4%.

Explain how land use change might lead to a rise in carbon dioxide levels in the atmosphere.

....

....

....

....

....

....

7   Explain why the cutting down of mature forest will not lead to a rise in CO_2 levels, until the trees are burnt.

....

....

....

....

Exercise 9.5 The need for the sustainable management of nature

Your work up to this point will have shown you how important the natural world is, both for its own sake and for continued human existence on Earth. This exercise helps you to bring together some of those points and to prepare for the final section on the strategies that we can use to protect the natural environment.

1 Explain the difference between a carbon sink and carbon store.

  ....

  ....

  ....

  ....

2 Name the process by which trees cause water to be added to the atmosphere.

  ....

3 Whale watching is a form of ecotourism. In 2009, a report gave the numbers of people who went on whale watching trips by country. This information is summarised in the table for the top ten countries.

USA	4 899 809
Australia	1 635 374
Canada	1 165 684
Canary Islands	611 000
South Africa	567 367
New Zealand	546 445
China	307 000
Argentina	244 432
Brazil	228 946
Scotland	223 941
Total for top ten	10 429 998
GLOBAL TOTAL	12 977 218

Complete the bar chart using information from the table.

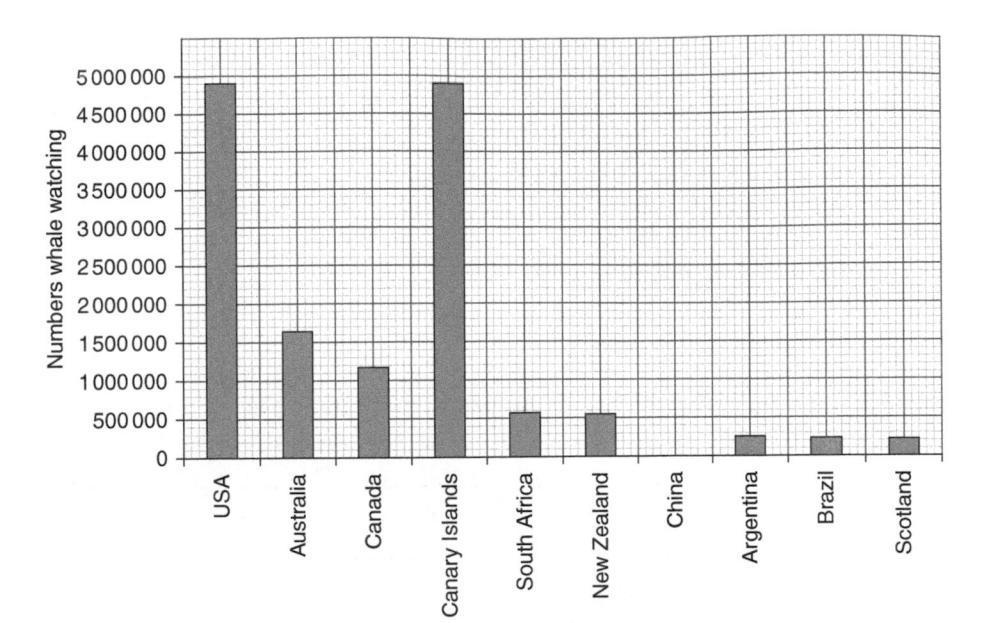

4 What percentage of global whale watching is carried out by the top ten countries?

....

5 The figure below shows the growth in tourism over the turn of the 21st century.

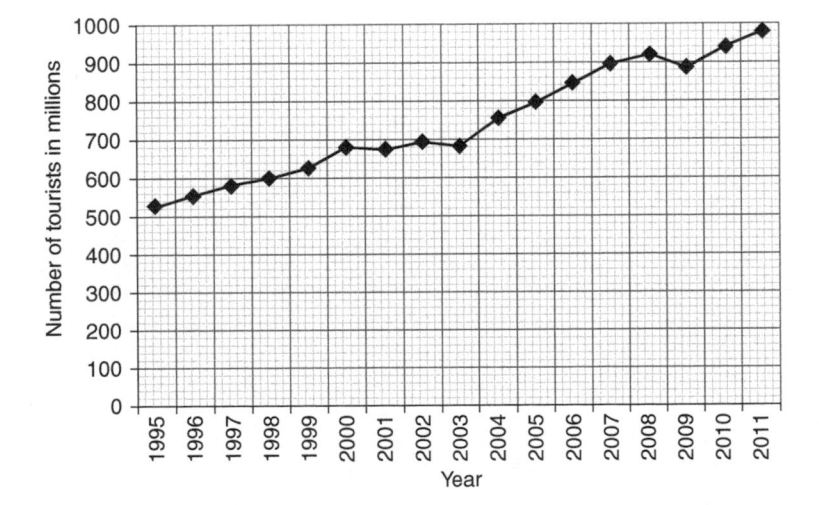

Describe the trends shown in the graph.

....

....

....

....

....

6 Suggest the likely environmental consequences of the trend you have described.

....

....

....

....

....

7 Suggest **three** ways in which any undesirable consequences of the changes in tourism over this time might be reduced.

....

....

....

....

....

Exercise 9.6 Strategies for conserving the biodiversity and genetic resources of natural ecosystems

> In this final section, the many and varied ways in which ecologists and environmental managers attempt to protect nature are addressed. In this exercise you will be able to think about a variety of these methods in various contexts.

1 'One strategy for the conservation of biodiversity of an ecosystem is the sustainable harvesting of wild plants and animals.'

   Explain what is meant by the word sustainable in the context of this sentence.

   ....

   ....

   ....

   ....

   ....

2 Explain how agroforestry can be considered as sustainable.

   ....

   ....

   ....

   ....

3 Rubber is grown mainly in either a mixed situation with other plants (called jungle rubber) or in a monoculture, with rubber trees only. Jungle rubber produces 590 kg / hectare/year, whereas monoculture produces 1310 kg/ha/year.

   Calculate how many times more productive monoculture is than jungle rubber.

   ....

4 Another way of cultivating rubber is called the rubber agroforestry system (RAS). Rubber trees are grown along with bananas, other fruit trees, maize, upland rice, grasses and legumes. Such a system is described as a 'strategy for conserving biodiversity and genetic resources'. Explain how this might benefit farmers and the environment.

....

....

....

....

....

5 Explain how a wildlife corridor might help to conserve biodiversity.

....

....

....

....

6 Explain why a government would decide to set up a seed bank rather than conserve living plants.

....

....

....

....

....

7 The map shows some important wildlife areas which contain similar species. Modify the map to show how the provision of wildlife corridors could improve the conservation of these species.

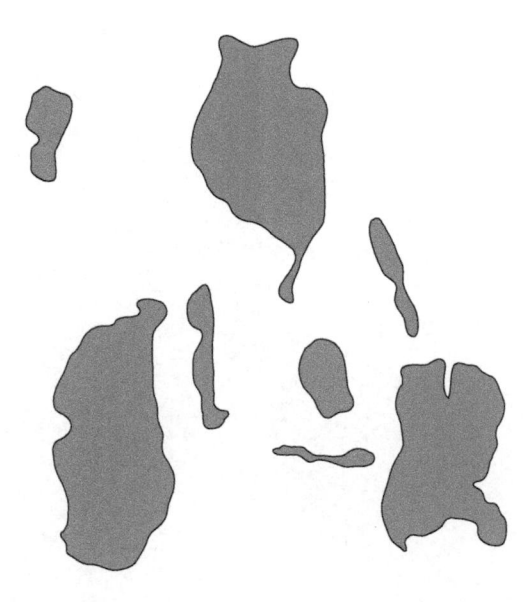

8 Explain the meaning of the term 'extractive reserve'.

....

....

....

....

9 The below diagram shows a simple diagram of a biosphere reserve. Name zone A, B and C.

....

....

....

....

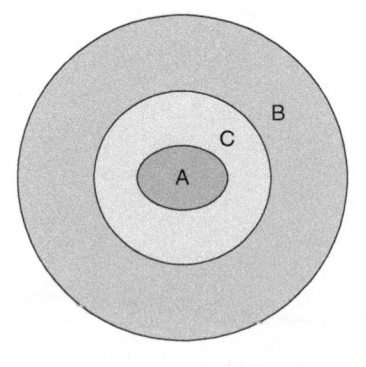

10 Describe the distribution of biosphere reserves in the world using the map.

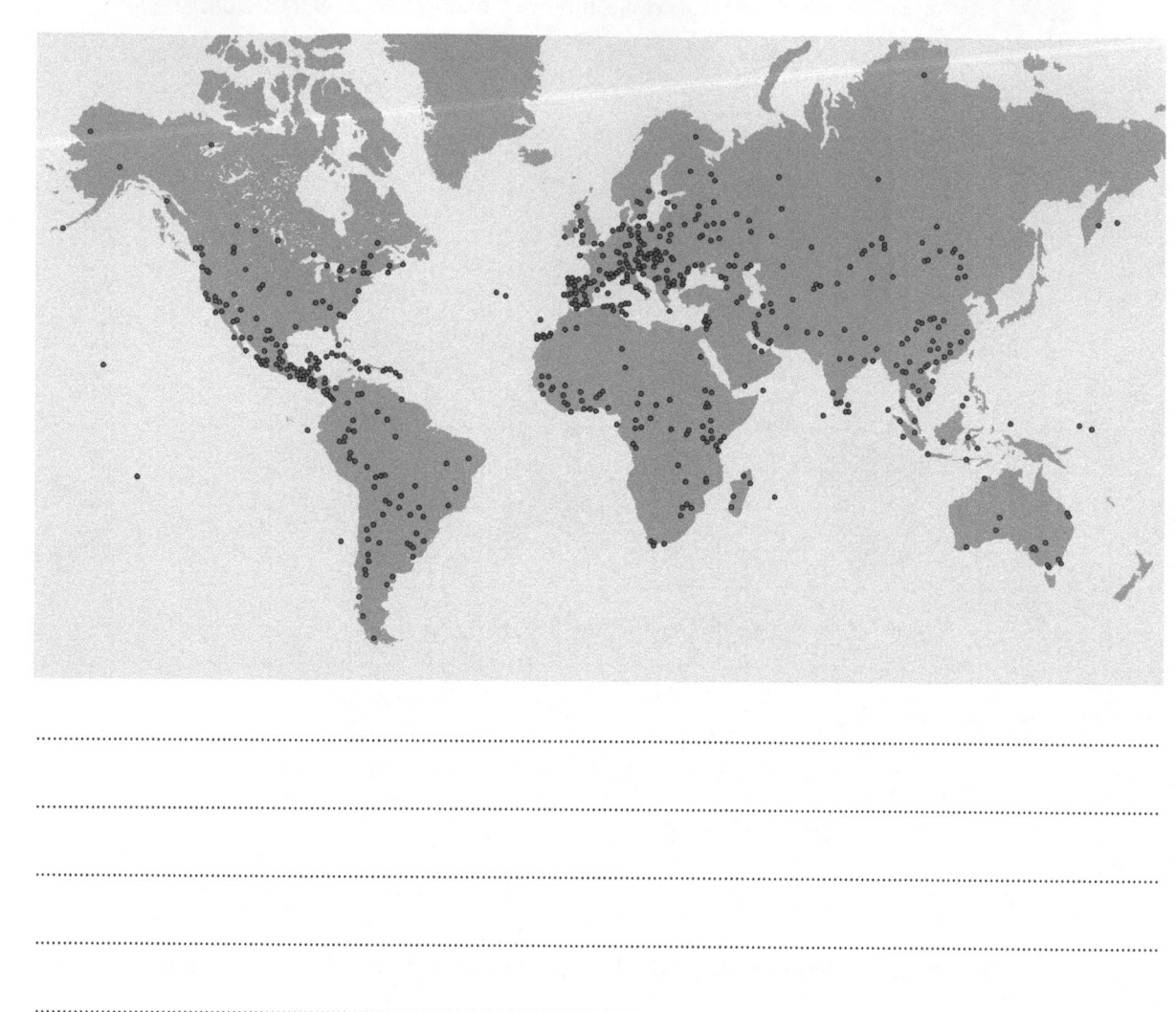

....

....

....

....

....

....

11 In Africa there are 70 biosphere reserves in 20 countries. Calculate the average number of reserves per country in Africa.

....

b The diagram below shows a drawing of the global seed bank on the island of Svalbard, part of Norway, in the Arctic Circle. Use your own knowledge and the information in the drawing to suggest why this site and design is suitable.

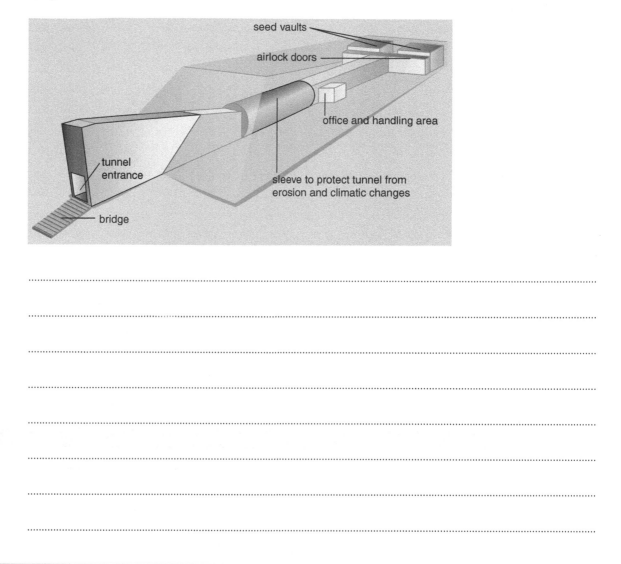

....

....

....

....

....

....

....

....

12 Calculate what percentage of the world total of 669 biosphere reserves are in Africa.

....

13 Zoos maintain a studbook for many of the animals they have. Explain the uses that they, and others, may make of such a studbook.

....

....

....

....

....

14 The table shows a breakdown of the seed stored in global seed banks by type of crop.

Type of crop	Percentage stored in seed bank
Cereals	53%
Legumes	13%
Vegetables	11%
Grasses used for grazing cattle (forage)	7%
Fruits and nuts	6%
Industrial crops	6%
Others	4%

a Plot this information in the form of a pie chart.

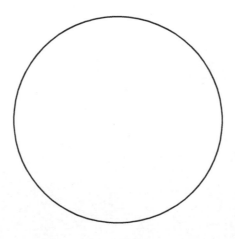